© Copyright Ca. All rights reserved. No portion of this book can be reproduced without expressed permission from the author.

Studio Baby
Adventures of a TV Reporter Turned Stay-at-home Mom

By Camaron Brooks

This book is dedicated to my loving husband, Donald for his constant support (how did I get so lucky?), to my parents Oscar and Janet for giving me so much love and encouragement, and for my children—my greatest teachers. Brandon, Addy and Corbin I love you so much!

The Rundown

Introduction
The A-Block
Chapter 1: Contraction, Contradiction
Chapter 2: Enlightened, Engorged and Feeling Not-So-Gorgeous
Chapter 3: Poopin' Ain't Easy
Chapter 4: Fly, Fly Baby
Chapter 5: My Clunker
Chapter 6: Process
Chapter 7: P.A.ying Dues
Chapter 8: Gifts Worth Giving
Chapter 9: #newsgiving
Chapter 10: Maybe this is too Personal
Chapter 11: Word Up
Chapter 12: Either the Start of a Really Bad Joke or My Real Life...
Chapter 13: Fear and Judgement
Chapter 14: Learning from My Losses
Chapter 15: Connection
Chapter 16: Ode to My Ladies
Chapter 17: Tunnel Vision
Chapter 18: Casting a Villain
Chapter: 19 Vision Boards and My Non-Linear Life
Chapter: 20 Milk, Cookies and a Selfie
Chapter 21: ALL CAPS, SIDS and the Semi-colon in the Room
Chapter 22: Lifelines, Deadlines & Million Dollar Dreams
Chapter 23: Write Tight
Chapter 24: Projectile Peas

The B-Block
Chapter 25: Need the loo, eh?
Chapter 26: Poverty
Chapter 27: My Default
Chapter 28: Our Vows
Chapter 29: Hollywood
Chapter 30: Glass Houses
Chapter 31: Love Layers
Chapter 32: Move Fresh
Chapter 33: Pixie Dust
Chapter 34: It Could Be Worse
Chapter 35: I Must Fuss
Chapter 36: Letter to Me at 13
Chapter 37: Everything Must Go
Chapter 38: Dumb Love
Chapter 39: Do you really think so?
Chapter 40: High, Low
Chapter 41: Not the End of the World
Chapter 42: No Youtube for You
Chapter 43: Emotional Credit Score
Chapter 44: Determination
Chapter 45: Letter to Brandon
Chapter 46: I'll always have NATS
Chapter 47: Ever Happily After
References
About the Author
Acknowledgements
Kicker: An Afterward About Thrills, Frills, and Wishes
Kicker #3: Life's Full of Surprises
Bonus Material

The A-Block

Introduction:

Inside a Barnes & Noble Starbucks, three years ago I quizzed my friend and former co-worker about motherhood. Her wisdom and know-how astounded me. *She knew so much.* I felt like an amateur trying to burp a gassy baby in her presence. She also taught me a lot about TV news in the months I filled in as her co-anchor on a top-rated, Emmy-winning morning show in the Texas Rio Grande Valley. She coached me, then and now. I tried to convince her to write a book. She said, "No, no you'll get there too. You just need to go through it."

I started recording my experiences days before Brandon was born. It was a sort of modern day rite of passage into motherhood. Naturally, it began as a blog. I felt the urge to write down everything I'd uncovered about life and myself. Lessons I hoped to teach my unborn son. *Lessons I still need to learn*. A new glaring bright light was shining down on my choices, attitudes, and moods even though I'd moved far away from the TV lights to which I'd grown so accustomed. I couldn't see my toes and I didn't know myself anymore. Swapping an old dream for a new one also challenged my sense of self. *I needed to go through it. I am glad to report I can see my toes again for the second time around but it won't be long.* I've never felt more at ease in my own life (even though my tootsies need a pedi I can't really afford).

The universe delivered a whirlwind of change in 2013 and our lives keep spinning. We welcomed our daughter in 2015 (the year this book was originally published as an ebook).

Dr. Dan Siegel and Tina Payne Bryson deliver some powerful tools to help me deal with my emotions post TV news and post-pregnancy (round one, two AND drum roll....Now I'm on pregnancy number THREE!). In *Whole Brain Child* they encourage parents to teach children to name their emotions. Siegel and Bryson call it their "name it to tame it" theory. The authors say we need to identify our emotions to calm ourselves down—different than venting or complaining, which involves blame. (Example, "I hate when Brandon throws food. He needs to learn some manners!" versus "When Brandon throws food I feel helpless. I can't seem to find a strategy to teach him to stop." See the difference?)

Another divine concept from the book explains kids and parents need to "move it" so they don't lose it. I've done jumping jacks in the kitchen during a difficult afternoon with Brandon. It worked. He giggled, and I lightened up.

I still can't believe my baby is a toddler turning into a boy. I documented his first year and edited during my pregnancy with Addison. I also worked part-time for a non-profit up until Addy's debut. Someday, I'll read these words with nostalgia. By then, Brandon and his sister may be tired of my stories. I've kept it mostly PG-13, just in case they decide to read them. Take me out for coffee and I'll fill you in on the jumbo-sized pads and other gross stuff about motherhood every new mum needs but doesn't want to hear about.

Like motherhood small market television is exhausting, exhilarating, and often overwhelming. Time seems to bend even more quickly under the duties of motherhood.

I spent more than 5 years working as a reporter in Texas. I met scores of people. Time moved swiftly and yet so very slowly. Contracts can feel oppressive—I wanted to move on to the next place and the next market. It's a shame I didn't enjoy the days more fully. I don't want to make the same mistake on this new adventure. I hear the echoes of my old fears and feelings from my younger, former colleagues. As women, they want a roadmap—like I did. They want to know they'll lead full lives with partners, kids and amazing careers. I didn't have a crystal ball either. (Although, I will share my encounter with Ms. Jennifer in Chapter 12. She claimed to see my future on coffee grounds.) I know I am not alone when I say I need to work on enjoying the moment, having a little faith, cutting myself some slack and accepting change.

News reporters definitely see change. I miss those exceptional moments when everything clicked or when I stood on the frontlines of something historic or special. My life is naturally much different now. The pace is a whole lot slower and a whole lot faster still. I miss my co-workers and I miss sharing stories of real people. Perhaps that's another reason for me to share mine. Writing feels like an old, cozy pair of sweatpants. I usually lounge and enjoy them around the house. Lately, I feel brave enough to wear them in public.

Speaking of going out, I went back to the same Barnes & Noble (almost two years to the day of meeting my friend with my bouncing baby boy). This time in 2015 she met Addison and I didn't need coaching. I wore a dirty old hat and tennis shoes. I took a break from our community rummage sale to catch-up.

We talked, laughed and I enjoyed the chance to honestly connect with someone who understands the grace, beauty and challenges of being a mom.

I left the book store feeling more confident than ever. I'm definitely growing into a more realistic, grounded and happy person. Although, I must tell you at least once a week I put my underwear on inside out, pray for strength, and remind myself I'm illiterate in at least 200 languages. The switch from newsroom to nursery was full of joys, budgets, lulls, mishaps and 90's rock ballad lullabies sung off-key. People share their stories in order to make sense of them. I very much wanted to make sense of my new life.

Throughout the book I consciously write *I* instead of *you*, whenever possible. That's because I am talking about *my insecurities and my fears*. I am sure you have your own. This book is a little like time traveling, I write in the present tense through the experiences as they unfolded for me as a new mom. I've included an affirmation, "takeaway" or a set of questions at the end of each chapter to help us both deepen our self-understanding. I realized my search for joy and stillness will be a life-long practice and pursuit. My sincere hope is these stories are relatable, humorous and helpful.

Live from Studio Baby, *Camaron Brooks*

Chapter 1: Contraction, Contradiction

"Peace is a daily, a weekly, a monthly process, gradually changing opinions, slowly eroding old barriers, quietly building new structures." – John F. Kennedy

It's 4:00pm on a Thursday afternoon in September. I am balancing mild contractions and boredom. Let's not forget joy and fear. Before my pregnancy I was a working TV reporter and anchor. It was a life-long dream I'd only begun to realize. I wanted to work on the Today Show. Well, a long time ago I did. ABC's 20/20 sounded fun too. I love writing and interviewing people and I wanted to prove my worthiness in this world.

I found some success while working on a morning newscast for a TV station along the Texas/Mexico border. Just about the time my childhood dream started to feel more like a burden; I started thinking about another childhood dream— having a family. I was like Marissa Tomei in her Oscar winning role as Mona Lisa Vito in the 90's movie *My Cousin Vinny*. My biological clock was [foot stomp] "ticking like this!" I feared I would never get pregnant, as women in their thirties sometimes do. I also feared I would never meet someone I loved enough to marry. I did meet an amazing man and I did get pregnant. Both surprised me. We decided to stop using birth control—I was convinced it would take years to conceive. It took 5 weeks. I left my job to join Donald in San Antonio, TX. He was transferred there for work and I was six months pregnant.

We were newlyweds who hurried our plans along because of baby. Leaving felt so easy— I love my husband and I love our unborn son. I am <u>ready</u> for this next phase.

I *wished* for this! I *prayed* for this! So why, does every contraction in this moment make me feel like I am saying goodbye to my old life and my old dreams? Aren't these dreams like an ex-boyfriend I don't really care about but don't want to see move on without me?

I've watched more news and tracked the twitter trends more now than I ever did while working in the TV news industry. I am sure once the baby comes (in a few hours or possibly in a few days) I will be too busy to have an identity crisis. In this moment, I wonder how many other mothers feel this way. If I stay home I'll feel guilty I am not earning my way in this world, even if my husband is supportive. If I go back to work I may end up handing over those little moments, like my baby's first smile, to a caregiver. The last trimester of my pregnancy served as a test run for staying home. It was nice at first, then boring and then downright maddening.

I thought I'd enjoy walking the mall and drinking lattes but when you don't have a job, shopping isn't all that fun and caffeine is pretty much a no-no for pregnant women. I *have* been writing, not as much as I'd like but I've also read a lot and yes I'll admit I've watched a fair amount of news and daytime TV. I've also nested. In 21st century terms this means the nursery is ready and I've updated all of my social media pages. I am now listed as a writer and former TV Reporter/Anchor.

I am still navigating, what this new title really means to me. I haven't published anything. I've talked about publishing. I've even written some children's books. I put a novella on hold. I've contacted an editor but as new parents, my husband and I can't really afford to fund what amounts to a hobby, at least not yet.

I am not sure getting back into news is the right answer either. I don't want to deal with long, stressful and demanding hours. I want to be home for dinner not covering a flood or hurricane. Those are definitely, reasons enough for a new mom to stay far away. I thought I'd give substitute teaching a try but by the time the staff entered me into their district-wide system the contractions started. The last thing I want is to slip in a middle school hallway because my water just broke. My husband convinced me the humiliation wasn't worth the $75 bucks anyway. So, I am at home riding out the waves of discomfort while confronting some equally uncomfortable feelings.

I doubt my mother felt this way. Although, hers was the first generation to believe they "could have it all." My generation understands this is myth yet we cling to this unrealistic notion whenever we're asked to give up something. I don't know why I feel the urge to pin recipes, tweet with important people, be the best mom, or the perfect wife and write the next great American novel.

As a girl I was taught to achieve, to raise my hand and answer questions in class, to volunteer, to seek out internships and network. Every single one of my girlfriends is asking herself "What's next? How do I get to the next level?"

The men I know don't live this way (at least not every waking moment of their lives). In college, the expectations only grew for me as a woman.

I felt I needed straight A's, sleek hair and a perfect body. Women pursue higher education while wearing even higher pumps.

I am not the first woman to analyze these great expectations. It's been discussed over and over again, probably just today on The Talk or The View.

So why, can't I let it go? Why can't I just settle for happiness? Isn't that what life is about? Why do I feel the urge to achieve more, to be more, to learn more, and to do more?

My husband doesn't feel this kind of pressure. My brothers don't feel burdened by societal expectations. They're happy! My husband for example jogs and plays soccer because it's fun. He reads magazines and watches sports because they interest him. He laughs because things are funny. I read self-help books, I follow Oprah and Deepak Chopra on twitter, I attempt to meditate, I know exactly two yoga poses and perform them religiously, and I obsessively read news articles to stay informed. (Just in case I should run into a lawmaker who wants my opinion on the crisis in Syria.) I work out so I don't get fat. Boy, oh boy I am glad I am giving birth to a son. Being a woman is exhausting. In this quest for balance I've tipped the scales in the wrong direction.

I wouldn't trade what I have now for anything. I just hope in this next phase I will give up trying to please everyone especially the naïve little girl inside of me who wanted to be a reporter, actor, veterinarian, doctor and first female POTUS. I suppose I am afraid I'll disappear if I don't keep up. If I am not a reporter/anchor who am I? BTW, these contractions keep coming. Can't I just believe I am enough without any achievements or social status? After all, I am a human worthy of love. I know I will love my son even if a dirty diaper is his only accomplishment for the day.

These thoughts continue to swirl. I want to share but I worry even *my mommy identity crisis* is a little cliché. A yahoo search yields numerous articles about this phenomenon.

Perhaps, my husband's mid-life crisis will come in a few years.

Until then, I want to embrace how he navigates life. He doesn't worry. He takes things day by day. He's not concerned with who he'll be once he's a father. He doesn't obsess about how to be the best dad ever. Nor does he even think about how we'll stay connected in our new roles as parents. He's taking this experience in stride.

I want a little piece of that peace. I want to savor these moments. I just hope I can give up on all the trappings of my gender, generation and up-bringing. Being liked. Being desired. Being perfect. Being amazing. Being unstoppable. Being Beyoncé, never skipping a beat. I need to work on just *being*. Like right now, what am I doing? I am writing mid-contraction. Maybe it's time I slowed down. Maybe it's time I realized I don't have that much time. The labor pains will pass and so too will my son's childhood. I can no longer cling to an identity constructed around my job but I never should have let "who I am" get so entwined with my career. It's too one dimensional anyway. I am more than that. We're all more than that. I am just riding these waves and praying I am strong enough to embrace happiness over perfection and love over the perception of success.

*Update Brandon was born two days later on the last day of summer 2013.

Affirmation:

I pick peace. Each day I let go of the need to be perfect. This simple decision adds more joy to my life.

Chapter 2: Enlightened, Engorged and Feeling Not-So-Gorgeous

"All those clichés, those things you hear about having a baby and motherhood - all of them are true. And all of them are the most beautiful things you will ever experience." –Penelope Cruz

It's raining clichés in the Brooks household. I'm pecking on the keyboard with one hand; my baby is asleep in the other. Let me make this brief. I just showered and the evening news is on.

Brandon is six days old and he's already witnessed my transformation from career woman to struggling new mother, complete with frizzy hair and frumpy pants. Who knew labor would be the easy part? I've laughed, cried, counted poops, dealt with urine showers, spit-up dreams and oh yeah I am leaking. I am totally in this moment, engorged breasts and all. I've heard it countless times: "Your life will change forever once you have kids. Sleep when the baby naps and accept help!" My little man was born exactly 6 days ago and all those axioms are spot on. I thought I loved my husband before D-day but now we're truly partners in something bigger than balancing a checkbook. He coached me through six and half hours of active labor without an epidural. I later found out he was holding back tears while helplessly watching me writhe on the hospital bed.

I thought I knew love. I thought I knew fear. Nothing is more terrifying than loving a defenseless little human. Did I buy the right car seat? Did I read enough? Life is fragile—this I know.

Most of the time, I block out those fears and just get through the day without considering the beauty of each breath without taking time to consciously breathe.

Listening to my son breathing in the dark from his bassinet is overwhelming. What if he just stops? It happens. I've heard the stories. I've reported them too. Just when I think I can't stand another nanosecond he takes another calm breath. It's a cocktail of absolute joy and unimaginable fear. (Of course, that's the only cocktail I've had in 9 months. So, it's pretty stiff.) It's a pit of terror and faith is the only light in the deep. It may be cliché but everything really is different now. And as the saying goes, I plan to enjoy the ride. (Tomorrow I will worry about fitting back into my old clothes.)

> Reporter's Notepad:
>
> How do you deal with life-changing experiences? What phrases or ideas have helped you get through new and challenging times?

Chapter 3: Poopin Ain't Easy

"Our fatigue is often caused not by work but by worry..." –Dale Carnegie

My husband went back to work today after spending two weeks off helping me adjust to life with our son. I miss his extra hands already. I am dodging bowel blowouts and trying to calm my anxiety. I found my worries piled higher than stacks of debris and tree limbs ready for pickup. We took our first walk alone. I clutched the stroller and felt hyper-aware of every speeding car and every perceived danger lurking seemingly steps away. I worried about mosquitoes and West Nile Virus. I worried the stroller might tip. I worried about the grooves in the gravel and all the jostling of my babies head. *I am the kind of mother I never wanted or thought I would be.*

Donald just looked at me wide eyed, when I told him about our adventures. Perhaps, this is a form of post-partum depression. I know I will get through it because I've experienced moments of bliss too. Gazing at my son or smelling his mostly bald little head vanquishes my negativity—at least for the moment. Learning to live in the moment is a lifelong struggle. I too easily get sucked into the dread or fantasy of the future or the comfort and nostalgia of the past.

As a kid, I used to dread every possible disaster to try to prevent it from happening. I believed I could spare my family suffering if I thought about the worst case scenario. It occurred to me at a young age that life unfolded in only unexpected ways, ways I could never even imagine. Maybe that's why all these thoughts are swarming like buzzards now.

I desperately want to control the world around me. I want to keep my son safe. Author, Speaker and TED talk guru Brené Brown talks about vulnerability and courage in her book *Daring Greatly*. She studies shame and the concept of foreboding joy. I so have that. Brandon brings me immense joy. Yet, I am terrified I *can't* protect him from everything in the world.

After all, how can you avoid brain-eating amoebas without missing out on slip-and-slides and lakes? After dinner, I decide to strap Brandon back into his stroller for another walk and (in lieu of the proverbial "chill pill" my father always recommends I take deep breaths.)

I have a choice—paranoid parent *or* the mother who will teach her son to live and love with all of his heart. Parenthood seems like the ultimate exit exam into adulthood. Everything I've learned up until now is getting tested. I must be better than I've ever been and on less sleep too. My little man's grown more than an inch and gained a pound since we left the hospital 18 days ago.

Growing is hard work. Sometimes he grunts and fusses while eliminating all the milk I've given him. During a moment when he was particularly gassy, I leaned over and told my husband "Poopin ain't easy." We chuckled.

Neither is parenthood for that matter. But that's our job. He's not here for us, we're here for him. This is *his* childhood and I can't stifle or ruin it with too much worry. *Back to the meditation mp3's I go.* For now it may be pooping, next teething or something else. I must be ready to comfort my son through these first struggles, even if it means enduring the agony of watching him fuss or cry. That's what I am here for and no, it ain't easy.

> **Breakout Extra:**
>
> A clergyman in Brownsville, TX once told me during the blessing of the fleet of Gulf Shrimpers heading out for the season "Anxiety craves action. Prayer is action."
>
> **Takeaway:**
>
> Take action when stressed or worried. Take a walk, say a prayer or go for a drive and don't forget deep breathing. All these actions quell worry.

Chapter 4: Fly, Fly Baby

"There are only two lasting bequests we can hope to give our children. One of these is roots, the other, wings." –Johann Wolfgang von Goethe

    My little one turned 2 months old. This happened somewhere between packing away my maternity jeans, patting the bottom of a colicky baby and flying to California for my brother's wedding. He's napping right now out of my arms (small miracle) so I figured I would slam a few words onto the screen. Whew, it's been a while! My fingers are ready to waltz across the keyboard after weeks of ruminating. I am sure simply *thinking* will someday replace typing, at least for now this is my favorite dance. I find comfort in the sound of tapping keys and thankfully I don't have to use my two left feet.

I ask myself, what have I learned in eight weeks of parenting? Everything! Ha. Of course, I am being factious. I've learned it goes by fast. I've come to this conclusion thanks to my son who seemingly grows after every feeding. I must also thank the countless moms and dads who've come right up and told me so. There was the lovely nurse on the plane who has a gorgeous 24-year-old model daughter who's been dating the same guy for five years. I could see the glisten of hope in her eyes as she awaits grand babies.

    There was the nice mom, wearing her self-proclaimed "huge" 15-week-old with a few straps of fabric. There was also the young dad with two tween girls, the mom of five including a daughter expecting twins, all my aunts and of course my son's great grandmothers.

The look in my mother's eyes said it best when she saw me holding my *own* baby for the first time. I hear ya, it goes by fast. The other thing I've learned is that "prep work" is the best work. If I want to get dressed in the morning I must get everything ready at night. I am more likely to eat from a bowl of washed apples than wash as I go. Seriously, time is of the up most importance now. Long showers, long walks, long dinners... Yeah, right.

I've pretty much scratched the word from my vocabulary. The second thing I've learned is simple: everyone must make their own mistakes. I intended for my son to sleep in a bassinet, my little one had other ideas. I fear he'll become a horrible co-dependent because he's sleeping in our bed but I've decided to do what works. At this point, I am sleeping more so it's a blessing—not a curse.

It's the season of non-stop nursing, gas and realizations. I can only do what I can with what I have at any given moment. This brings me to Brandon's blowout on the airplane. Forget snakes! We're talking poop on the plane, on the onesie, on his pants, spilling out of the diaper and an hour left before landing. This would be scary for any mom, especially a new one. Thank the angels above for the woman sitting next to me. Strike that, she *is* an angel. She held Brandon's head while I changed him awkwardly. Us moms need to stick together, right?! I hope I can pay it forward when I get the chance.

I learned a lot on this trip including something I must have already known: if you're like me and have a good mother, you have no idea how much she's sacrificed for you. It's like ice skating along the wall. You feel like you're a pro when in reality it's always there to catch you when you stumble.

The wall should really take more credit but that's not the wall's style. Of course, modesty only goes so far. My mother was royally upset when my brother in eighth grade proclaimed "he practically raised himself."

I too always felt like I did so much on my own. In reality, my mother was that wall on which we all leaned. I still do. Now, I am mom and she filled me in on this secret. She told me everything I am experiencing is *normal*. She went through it too. She gave up so much to raise three strong independent children. She taught me how to make decisions and chase my dreams, even when moving away wasn't *her* choice for me. She is amazing. I knew this before but now I understand *why*. During the trip from Texas to California we talked about hemorrhoids, incontinence and stretch marks. She made mistakes (don't get me wrong) and I will too. I think the best gift I will try to bestow on my children, my mother certainly gave me—wings. Today, I am happy in my little nest knowing someday my son will fly his own way. Thanks to all the mothers and fathers out there reminding me how soon that day will come. Noted— I will enjoy all the lovely, tiring, amazing days I have left.

> Affirmation:
> My job as a mother involves three simple tasks; love, so my son will learn how to love and connect with others, inspire a love of learning, and build confidence so one day he can make his own decisions. It is not my job to shield my son from real-life or entertain him and bow to his every whim in order to keep him happy at all costs.

Chapter 5: My Clunker

"I'm proud of my body. I'm finally in a good place and learning to love me for me, and not somebody else's standards." –Khloe Kardashian

    My fingers dragged shampoo suds and hair away from my scalp like waves washing sea weed to shore. I looked down; a second clump of chestnut locks blocked the drain. So much for those prenatal vitamins, I thought. My experienced anchor friend told me this would happen after I gave birth. I would lose my hair and wouldn't recognize my body. *She was right again.*
    Sometimes I look in the mirror and don't recognize my face, either. After years of layering foundation with a trowel it's a refreshing change. I've never really obsessed about my looks. I can't count how many times I've sat on the anchor desk with lipstick on my teeth. I've also gone on the air with little or no makeup. I stopped the practice after I sent flooding coverage to a news director for feedback. He told me I needed to look more attractive if I ever wanted to find another TV job. I didn't take it personally. I listened. I went to a fantastic makeup artist in Midland, TX named Ashlee Rice at Let's Face It Makeup Studio. I begged her to teach me. She helped me make the most of my features. Soon after, I landed a new and better paying job.
    It's a world of rapid fire judgments and I picked an industry steeped in superficiality. A viewer once wrote in to tell me I looked like a cartoon Geisha. *She couldn't take me seriously.*

I laughed when I reviewed the air check. I forgot to blot my lip gloss. Oops. My bosses were required to sign off on all major hair changes and it was mandatory I wear a suit jacket every day for years. It's weird. Now, I feel like I am required to wear pajama bottoms until noon. I've hit a wall of self-acceptance I can't seem to climb. As a woman I am bombarded with messages urging me to strive for a better more toned body.

Settling for the body I was born with is akin to becoming a communist. I wish abs mattered to me. They don't. Breastfeeding in public doesn't either. I wear tennis shoes with jeans. I don't care what people think. Makeup is no longer a must, it's an extra. I do a few quick swipes of cover up and color and that's completely for me and for my husband.

On the topic of my husband; he can bench press the equivalent of me even with 5 to 10 extra pounds of baby weight still left on my frame. If he holds our son for 20 minutes his arms tire. My arms can go for hours. My body was made for motherhood. I don't recognize myself in the mirror anymore because I am so much stronger than I ever believed.

I see my body as a vehicle— a vector for love. This simile is a little trite but it makes so much sense now. I hauled my son to the studio and to water aerobics and to a George Strait concert all before he needed an infant carrier. My body takes me great places just like some of the old clunkers I drove around in college.

In my old Volvo I needed to replace a fuse if I wanted to roll down a window. That didn't matter much because that car got me to and from the gorgeous Southern California coast.

My body may bear a few more dents and dings, so what? I sometimes find pimples on my derriere and hairs hanging out of my nose.

My nipples may float like UFO's much lower on my chest and the skin on my stomach is like a 90's hair scrunchie tied around my belly button. I am human without my body I wouldn't be here. Neither would Brandon.

A few years back I started a practice I still continue as often as I can remember. I say thanks to my body for all it's done for me throughout the day. I try to give myself nightly foot rubs, too! During my reporter days my body often went without adequate water and ran solely on fast food. After a few years of that kind of abuse I gained 30 pounds. I didn't lose the weight by hating my body or through deprivation. I lost the weight with kind regard for the job my heart, lungs and body perform with ease (health is the truest blessing).

My new regimen included walking and swimming. I listened when I ached. I added something fresh to every meal. I cut down on soda. I didn't force myself to eat everything on my plate. I picked up *this practice* during a visit to the Czech Republic to visit my dear friend and former foreign exchange student. She looked amazing and I wanted her secret. She told me she never cleared her plate. It took a year but my body thanked me. So far, I've lost most of the baby weight by implementing the same plan. I plank when my son does tummy time. I walk. I hold and bounce him for hours. And, I say thanks for making a miracle.

I hear so many friends and loved ones castigating their bodies for bulges only they can see. I say the best hugs come from imperfect bodies. I doubt Gisele is a good hugger and I bet she hates something about herself.

It is physically impossible to embrace happiness without deepening smile lines. The beauty and power of each wave forever rewrites the shore. Me, I'd rather laugh now than look flawless in a casket later. If I am lucky, one day I'll only find strands of gray at the bottom of the tub. *I want to live long enough to see some grandkids and to write and see the world.* I will only get there by accepting my so-so self and taking care of me. A joyful smile and dim lighting is all anyone really needs to look sensational, anyway. (If anyone tries to serve me a croissant....you know I'll say yes!)

> Affirmation:
>
> I will find times throughout the day to thank my body for its beautiful work. I love the feeling of walking on my own two feet. I love extending my arms to tickle or hug my son. I am grateful I am able! As far as my husband is concerned—a good shave, a salt scrub and dim lighting really do make all the difference.

Chapter 6: Process

"If the path be beautiful, let us not ask where it leads." — Anatole France

Moms need mantras. One thing at a time. Don't sweat the small stuff. Feel the fear and do it anyway (that's one of my favs). I find these phrases coax me through thickets of physical and emotional exhaustion. I was able to piecemeal my latest mantra from an interview I saw with famed Buddhist Monk Thich Nhat Hanh. I now try to draw upon these words whenever I am feeling overwhelmed: *Here I am, walking into this brand new moment, engaged and in love with the beautiful and mysterious process of life.* I breathe. I say it twice if needed. It occurs to me that my life is a parade of forgettable seconds, strung up like popcorn garland. Minutes, hours and eventually years become separated only by bright flashy cranberries. My eyes once fixated on those special occasions; birthdays, weddings, graduations, and vacations dangling red on the line. Those pops of color make life exciting but growth doesn't happen there. It starts with a single thought in a boring insignificant moment just like this one. *It's a process.*

Process fascinates reporters. In the TV news arena it's a brand of storytelling meant to show viewers the steps needed to develop a story. In the movies it's the montage.

You know...The clips highlighting the hero or heroines journey to overcome the odds, lose weight, or snag the job of their dreams. I adore a good montage. (Rocky running up those iconic steps in Philly while Survivor's "Eye of The Tiger" blares in the background—gets me every time.)

Montages inspire. Montages make it look easy. Right now, I want to waste time picking out the perfect song for some hypothetical montage starring Katherine Hagel as me. (Only kidding) I know better. Success comes to those who learn to find pleasure in the creative process needed to get the job done. Enter another mantra: Now isn't the time for rewards, it's time for work.

I visited my old TV station and met up with former friends and colleagues. I can't tell you how good it felt to hear them ask about the process of taking care of my baby boy. *Thanks for asking.* I've found the process of parenting is one of elimination (really, my son eliminates all day long.) Ok seriously, is he wet? *No.* Is he hungry? *No.* Is he tired? *No.* Is there a hair somehow wrapped around his toes or penis? *Yes.* Sometimes it's a long process. Mystery solved for now. It's a merry go round of problem solving—spinning 24 hours a day, every day. I could throw away these everyday moments and focus only on the milestones but I'll tell you, as a mom, I want to hold onto every kernel. The upset, unsettled moments show me glimmers of my son's resolve. His inquisitive nature pops out every time he grabs for whatever I am holding. I gladly eat up those everyday moments with pleasure. Before Brandon I heard "live for the moment" packaged in a thousand ways. You will hear me say it again and again; *I haven't learned this lesson but I am trying*. And I will keep trying.

In tough moments, when I react calmly I teach patience. In weak moments if I choose patience I model perseverance. I must remember the things I teach if I am not patient—if I am not persevering.

The process of writing and re-writing gives me more enjoyment than the final product these days. My right hand thumb is pecking these words onto an email I'll send to myself on my smart phone. My left hand is busy keeping Brandon's sleeping head from slouching in his car seat while my husband drives us back to San Antonio. Which brings me to the best question I heard on the trip: Is there anything I can't do with one hand? Absolutely not! *Here I am, driving into the here and now. With this breath I embrace the miraculous procession of seconds that will one day make up my whole beautiful and exceptional life.*

> Reporter's Notepad:
>
> What is your creative process?
>
> How can you embrace creativity without worrying about the finished product?
>
> How can you make more time for creativity in your life?

Chapter 7: P.A.ying Dues

"You got to pay your dues if you want to sing the blues...And you know it don't come easy." -Ringo Starr

The unmistakable stink of ballpoint pen followed me from the studio to the craft services table. I refilled the candy bowl and straightened a stack of napkins before power walking into the production office. "Everywhere I go...I smell ink," I said with disgust. Another production assistant trailed behind. "I think your pen exploded."
What?? The pen I couldn't find earli...oh my God it's in my hair! AND ALL OVER MY NECK. "Your uh..." another crew member pointed to the leaky pen poking through my messy ponytail. My fingers already bore the sticky blue proof. I could hear the director calling for me. "Makeup!"
Ridiculous things happened while working as a production assistant. I locked my keys in the car three times. I dropped a bag of burgers meant for the hosts of the show. I misspelled the executive producers name while making a Starbucks run. Yet, I survived (figuratively, of course). Another P.A. literally survived a car fire on the 405 Freeway while picking up a vintage vehicle for a taping.
I met the hosts of the show while working at Papalucci's Ristorante (one of my favorite jobs ever). The twins were east coast mechanics working on a reality TV competition show in 2004. Each twin mentored a pair of car enthusiasts. The teams worked on identical vintage cars before drag racing each other at a track north of Los Angeles. The winners drove both cars home afterwards.

The production company paid me a daily rate and the hours dragged like the races (sometimes stretching to 14 or 16 hours a day). I worked constantly, keeping my serving job four nights a week and washing wardrobe in my off time.
Full Throttle operated on a budget this gave me some great opportunities.

By my second week I was ordering catering, organizing wardrobe, and helping with makeup and anything else the crew needed. I wanted to pattern myself after a company big-wig I saw ironing on my first day. *She did what needed to get done.* A professor once told me to do even the small jobs well, if I wanted people to remember me for the big ones. This still applies to TV news and pretty much any job. Back on that *blue* day, I wiped my hands and grabbed a loose powder compact. I jogged toward the director who sounded annoyed. "Your neck?" he looked puzzled.

"My pen exploded" I said calmly as I patted powder on one of the twins. I wanted to dive into the candy bowl I'd just replenished. I stayed put. I could handle this. Another P.A. showed up with an alcohol wipe. He held it up as if asking for permission to swab. A tacit eye swap...swab away!

Blue and bright days pass the same. After hours with ink residue in my hair and on my neck I walked out of the studio with a group of production assistants. One of the guys spent the day running tapes from Long Beach to the main office in north of Los Angeles. "What did I miss?" We collectively shook our heads. "Why is your neck blue?" Sometimes laughter is the only choice.

It seems I am still paying dues. This time it's the entrance fee into the joys of parenthood. On several late night occasions Brandon's mustard yellow poop has flown over the changing table onto the floor. Pee has pelted my husband and me like a hose. Sticky white spit-up has run down our shirts. We can only swap shocked and exhausted giggles each time. These dues are already paying dividends. *It's comforting to know we're in this together.*

> Takeaway:
> It's important to learn to laugh at life's silly moments. The dues you pay now will be the stories you tell later.

Chapter 8: Gifts Worth Giving

"When I stand before God at the end of my life, I would hope that I would not have a single bit of talent left and could say, 'I used everything you gave me.'"
– Erma Bombeck

Two lovely young producers threatened everyone in the control room. "Don't say anything to Camaron!" The launch of their innovative new morning newscast would go smoothly in spite of me—an overly anxious anchor sitting on the desk. During rehearsals the lovelies noticed a correlation between compliments and my poor performance. *It was late breaking news to me.*

Looking back, I certainly have responded to criticism better than compliments over the years. After the initial sting of a critique I've often thought "I'll show them." Inversely, after the initial excitement of a compliment I've thought "can I keep this up?" Just as blocks start to sway the higher they're stacked, I feared I'd fumble and fall down along with the lofty expectations of others.

When it comes to writing, words seem to zip-line from a place deep inside of me. Taking credit feels like a sham. I can't take credit for my skin either. I'm blessed with two gorgeous grandmothers who doled out good genetics. "You don't even look tired" someone told me at my brother's wedding, six weeks after Brandon's birth. Four syllables: TV makeup. Gotta love HD Makeup Forever Professional. The No.5 palette sold at Sephora is the best. I've even downplayed compliments from strangers. "This shirt? Thank you, but I'll tell ya TJ Maxx. Paid $10 dollars."

Growing up, my family showed love through jokes. Neighbors on Euclid Street still hear the echoes of my mother's laughter. We made fun of each other and ourselves. *We still do*. My brother recently broke his fibula ice- skating. I only know this because I happened to see a Facebook post about how he should bow out of the Sochi Olympic Games. *He broke his leg*. I found myself joking about his accident when I checked on him too.

My parents never wanted my brothers and me to take ourselves too seriously. Instilling humility seemed to matter a great deal to them. It's understandable; we lived in California (heaven forbid we'd grow too big for our board shorts). They often reminded us with love; "there will always be someone faster, prettier, and smarter." I suppose I've carried those words for far too long, unknowingly, going through life swatting compliments like volleyballs. Last night, while listening to *A Return to Love* by Marianne Williamson those words replayed one last time before I released them. Her words helped me shed the old. "There is nothing enlightened about shrinking so that other people won't feel insecure around you. We are all meant to shine, as children do."

Three of my gorgeous and talented cousins demonstrated this attitude while singing in my parent's backyard the day after my brother's wedding in November. The impromptu concert and their lovely voices touched my grandmother. She teared up. My cousins didn't hold back. They didn't hoard their gifts. They didn't wait for a bigger or better audience.

Although, I am pretty sure they could have found a tequila bottle was placed on each table at the wedding the night before.

No, my cousins gave without expectation. *That's humility. Definitely a revamp on the lesson my parents taught me.* So, here are the words I want Brandon to carry with him as he heads into the world—no matter if he's a TV anchor, a welder or the POTUS: *You are a gift and you possess gifts; mine them, polish them and here's the important part my baby give those gems away.*

If only I'd learned this years ago. I could have saved several producers, a couple of news directors and a high school basketball coach a lot of headaches.

Reporter's Notepad:

How do you deal with compliments?

What is your gift or talent?

Can you share your God given gifts more freely?

What's holding you back?

Chapter 9: #newsgiving

"Write it on your heart that every day is the best day in the year." -Ralph Waldo Emerson

A tsunami of nostalgia followed a little note. A friend and former producer congratulated me on my new blog and the birth of my little man. Her sweet words reminded me of Saturday mornings spent feverishly stacking stories into the rundown and gabbing about when this day would come. "All of a sudden we're real adults," another friend wrote. I love how Thanksgiving gives us reason to reconnect and reminisce. Another reason to be grateful; this year, I didn't need to consult the holiday schedule. Although, I know I will miss walking into a dark and empty newsroom on Thursday.

I loved staring at a fresh rundown and deciding how to fill the holes. I loved coming up with story ideas for new reporters. I am convinced anyone can cover breaking news. The B-block story (after the first commercial break) was the story I loved to tell. My creativity ran free on slow days.

I wasn't always so self-assured. Take my first live shot. I stumbled and never recovered. I wanted to stick to the script and painfully so. A train slammed into a car, killing a man in Midland, Texas. A young reporter from the competing station was also new. We were desperate to impress our bosses. As I recall we both flopped—the start of a friendship. She's now a new mom, too. I've met some amazing people over the years. Photographers, reporters, interview subjects— I am so grateful.

I need to do a better job of staying connected.

Although, to me, once a friend always a friend even if I only stay up-to-date via the Facebook feed. The terrible live shots (yes, plural) turned out to be a metaphor for adulthood. I couldn't cling to my script. The job demanded flexibility. I needed to respond to the world around me. I learned I couldn't try to act like reporter—I needed to be myself as a reporter. I think this is true about life. During those early days, I was living like a college kid at night and an adult in the morning. Oh, the twenties! Oh, The Bar!

It took me some time to find more peace and balance. I must still cross a rickety footbridge on this journey toward mindful, intentional living each day. That doesn't mean I didn't have fun in the process. And that's the point. It's a process and a path I am still walking. My wise friend's note reminded me to enjoy this time with my husband and son more deeply than I enjoyed my past. This line from The Office sums it up, "I wish there was a way of knowing you were in the good old days before you've actually left them." As newsrooms across the country thin out and as airports and kitchens fill up, I pray all of my friends and dear family members enjoy wherever they find themselves.

> *Affirmation:*
>
> *I am learning to let go of the need for control, I focus on enjoying where I am right now. I embrace the joys and challenges of my life as it is in this moment.*

Chapter 10: Maybe this is too personal...

"The great motherhood friendships are the ones in which two women can admit [how difficult mothering is] quietly to each other, over cups of tea at a table sticky with spilled apple juice and littered with markers without tops." - Anna Quindlen

Poop just isn't my thing—I know I've written about it a lot lately. I just don't generally like the topic. I don't find poop jokes funny. I don't like bathroom themed products like poop diaries or Poo-Pourri in my stocking (sorry mom). In college, when in my presence, my roommates only referred to it as "the thing we do not speak of." Later in life, this translated into a disdain for dirty diapers. I refused to change a single one of my nephews' wet nappies. Yet, in my newest role, poop is automatically built into my day. It's unavoidable. I expected that. I didn't expect to spend so much time talking about my own poopscapades.

"You're really upset about the hemorrhoids!" One of my closest friends practically shouted as we drove my son around town. He slept. We gabbed. Win/Win. Yes, I'm upset! First, they hurt. Second, they fucking hurt! That's how my son heard his first F-bomb. Although, at the time I wasn't cursing about the pain but I'll get to that later.

Growing up, I heard every expletive in the book. My mother modeled a colorful vocabulary. My brothers wanted the freedom and power of the almighty curse word, too. My mom would even give them a minute to say whatever words they wanted.

The deal: refrain from using those words in public and start the timer. By 30 seconds the boys ran out of choice four letter words and usually said something ridiculous like "monkey balls" over and over.

I never really liked the flare of cussing. I liked to express myself using different and better words. Cursing in TV news can cost you heavily. Some may remember the infamous first and last day of A.J. Clemmente. He made the rookie mistake of believing his microphone was off. Microphones are always on. Clemmente dropped the f-bombs in Bismark, ND but it made news across the country. Just take a gander at You Tube. I knew better than to think I could cuss in my off time and not let a curse word slip when it counted. It's about being authentic—another reason for me to try to refrain from using those words. FCC or no FCC, as a new mom I was pretty adamant I didn't want my son to ever hear a bad word barrel out of my mouth. That is until the day after Thanksgiving. By the way, anyone looking for an evergreen day-after-thanksgiving (other than black Friday story) can just ride along with a plumber. It's one of the busiest days of the year for them. I knew this piece of trivia but I never thought I would live it.

I've dealt with issues in the bathroom department since my son's birth but I've been too preoccupied with my little one to solve my own problems. Then came Thanksgiving dinner and leftovers...oh Niña...Pinta and the Santa Maria, deliver me! I tell my good friend what happens next. My son is strapped into a bouncer outside of the bathroom. The door is open. I go—slowly and painfully. She's embarrassed for me. I am too just retelling this story. After a flush, the water starts rushing over. I run outside leaving my son belted into his bouncer. Bam! I get locked out.

Tears billowed from my eyelids. Come 'on! I am not wearing any shoes. I remember the spare key. I go back inside. The infected water floods the floor. I still don't have the plunger. Really, this is far too personal. I grab the plunger and give it a go. Then a flush and then more water rushes out and that's when I let the f-word glide off my tongue like a metal slide in the South Texas summer heat. My son starts screaming! He's never even heard me shout. He once startled and cried when I sneezed but that didn't count. I am sweating. My towels are soaked. I am still in pain and I decide to call my husband while holding a crying baby. The baby sounds like the combined sirens of a four alarm house fire. Finally, after my husband can't understand a word I am saying I tell him I need to calm down so I can calm the baby down. The lessons and reminders keep coming like water overflowing out of a toilet.

    My horrified friend just laughed at the hilarity of it all. I've been busy and haven't made as much time for friends. In this moment I realize how critical they are to my survival as a new mom. I didn't want to tell this story over the phone or at all. Frankly, I've even felt a little boring every time my friends call to update me on their lives. The question, "What did you do all day?" burns like...well, a hemorrhoid. Opening up about the good and the bad parts of my new life reminded me; life is full of both. Thank God for friendship. I am grateful to my dear friend for visiting and asking great questions, actually waiting to hear the response and for forgiving me. I know I've been lost in baby land. This isn't a fairy tale... not at all. It's better. It's my real life. Oh, and thanks to the plumber who made my house a stop on his day after Thanksgiving. I guess Brown Friday, doesn't have the right ring to it.

> Takeaway:
> There is a tendency with new moms to retreat into the duties of motherhood. Don't forget the importance of friendships.

Chapter 11: Word Up

"Without knowing the force of words, it is impossible to know more."
-Confucius

Nothing intimidated me more—pitching stories, every morning. Scribbling ideas into a box hoping one met my bosses' exacting standards. I improvised on the days I couldn't find much to fill my little square. I told anecdotal stories, hypothesized about any number of things and tried to *act cool.* On one such day I was going on and on about some mishap in the field when my tongue went rouge and out slipped an epic Freudian/Palinism. "It was a total kerfuckle....I mean kerfuffle!" I said awkwardly laughing, my face ruddy with embarrassment. I wished for a giant cane to yank me out of the newsroom. (I couldn't refudiate. I'd made a silly mistake.) So language evolves. Words are time capsules. Words represent entire movements (hello Occupy). Words bring down moguls (ahem, Paula Dean). Words change, charge and trigger hearts the way violence never can. Words mend. Words inspire. Words enrage. Words incite. Words create destinies. I choose my words carefully (at least most of the time.)

Don Miguel Ruiz wrote, what has become my personal bible, *The Four Agreements.* I read it while visiting the Czech Republic more than a decade ago. The first agreement: *be impeccable with your word* (means more than just honesty. For me it's about using words to elevate myself and others.)

The trip made my lifetime. One of the highlights was driving around in a red hot Dodge Viper. It belonged to my friend's father. Little boys actually ran after us on the unpaved streets (capitalism—that's the word that came to mind.)

Her dad manufactured bikes sold in China. Many people in her home country still drove around the old cars from the communist era. The only word I still remember in Czech—keg (soudek.) I am not proud to admit it but I taught my new friends an American *soudek*-stand.

Before I adopted non-regional diction for broadcast I tossed around the adverb hella a lot (yes, I grew up in NorCal.) Just hearing the word "hella" takes me back to the late 90's. My friends and I used this word to amplify just about everything. According, to urbandictionary.com "hella" originated on the streets of San Francisco. It's used in place of really or very (totally a time capsule).

We hold onto the words were given, especially as children. A study conducted by researchers Betty Hart and Todd R. Risley found kids in affluent homes hear more than a half million more words of encouragement than those in poor households (that's hella crazy!) A poor child will hear more than a *hundred thousand* more discouraging words than his rich classmates.

Recently, I've noticed I have Brandon's undivided attention when I am chatting on the phone. He listens to every word with *wonder* (like a private eye or a jealous boyfriend.) He hears everything including anything I say about myself. He pays attention to the types of words I use and the tone. Just more reason to keep it light and positive. Quoting my dad quoting Thumper from Bambi, "If you can't say anything nice don't say anything at all."

I want the words I use to matter. I want my son to trust my word. I want him to grow up hearing incredibly positive, encouraging words. If for some reason he messes up or misses the mark (and finds himself in the middle of a totally, hella crazy, out-of-control kerfuckle) I want him to hear me say, "I love you. I am here for you. Let's do better tomorrow."

> *Takeaway:*
>
> *Words matter. Use 'em don't abuse 'em! Think only positive thoughts; say only positive words (especially about and to yourself). Your self-talk creates your reality.*

Chapter 12: Either the Start of a Really Bad Joke or My Real Life...

"After all these years, I am still involved in the process of self-discovery. It's better to explore life and make mistakes than to play it safe. Mistakes are part of the dues one pays for a full life." -Sophia Loren

    A life coach, a therapist and a psychic walk into a *juice* bar... Just kidding, I went to see all three over the span of twelve months starting in 2010. The life coach helped me identify strategies for building my ideal life. The therapist uncovered a harmful set of mistaken beliefs. The psychic put me at ease. I paid $40 dollars for Miss Jennifer to read my future on coffee grounds. I guess I needed a stranger to tell me everything was going to be *okay*. She advised me to leave a dried-up relationship. She also saw a handsome husband and two kids dancing across the Folgers® original blend. Yippee! She told me I'd find more success in my second career (still waiting for *that* part of her augury to come true but hey.)

    Even after all I've learned I don't walk entirely in peace and faith all the time. Sometimes, a broadcast news crawl[†] scrolls on the lower third of my mind. Big bold letters read: not good enough, not smart enough, not funny or talented enough. Instantly, a surge of inferiority washes over my gut. I ran into this feeling when I watched writers pitch manuscripts to agents and publishers on twitter. I thumbed across trending topics during my son's nap and found #pitmad. Progress on my first novel halted during pregnancy. I assured myself I simply couldn't go into such a dark head space—*it could hurt the baby*. Probably, some latent fear of rejection in 140 characters or less played a part.

First dates, job interviews and confrontations often elicit similar storms of self-doubt. I once spent thirty minutes locked inside a bathroom in Big Spring, Texas after meeting then Governor Rick Perry at a press event. Sweat stripped most of my makeup and my knees trembled from all the high-class handshaking I was doing.

I practiced mindful breathing with wet paper towels under my armpits. Live shots often sent me into a nervous tailspin and I nearly missed my six o'clock hit. I literally pounded and begged to get out of the building like a repressed feeling. A janitor finally let me out. My meeting with then New Mexican Governor Bill Richardson went even worse. It started with an interview of a man wearing a golden cock (a doodle doo) around his neck during my second day on the job as a reporter covering the Midland-Odessa TV market. The coverage area included a portion of New Mexico.

In early 2007, a group of cock-fighting enthusiasts wanted answers. They told me Governor Richardson promised he wouldn't outlaw the sport during his bid for re-election. Not long after New Mexico became the 49th state to ban cockfighting. I pulled the trigger. I asked the question. "What would you say to all of the people outside who say you lied to them?" I honestly, can't remember his response. I remember the look on his face. I flushed like a little girl. I was twenty-four and a nobody. Isn't outlawing cockfighting a *good* thing, I thought? Poor cocks. I felt like a hen—a big fat chicken. I felt like an even bigger failure, imposter and all around idiot with a communications degree. Don't they hand those out at Starbucks?

You see why I *needed* Miss Jennifer. My therapist helped me unpack some of this baggage as well. I hitched all of my self-worthiness to intangibles like success. I needed more and more and more to feel adequate. Inner peace, like my writing continues to be a work in progress. I don't have a fancy title on which to hang my self-worth anymore. I am enough even if I remain at home with my son and never publish anything. *I am enough.* I know I must live it if I want my son to grow up knowing *he's enough.*

So, at first sight of insecurity bubbling to the surface I pull upon the strategies of a life coach, a therapist and a psychic. I affirm, I disabuse mistaken beliefs and I *trust that it's going to be okay*. I may not be ready for the next #pitmad but I will at least know I am worthy. (Bravo to all the brave souls willing to put themselves out there. Keep pitching.)

*words broadcast across the bottom of television screens, usually to convey some breaking news or weather information

---

Affirmation:

It's going to be okay! I will tell myself a thousand times until I believe it and I no longer need to hear it from anyone else.

Chapter 13: Fear and Judgment

"The more you judge, the less you love." –Mother Theresa

I dipped into a silk sleeping bag tucked into hard white sheets. Tears queued in the back of my throat as I flipped off a lamp in a small and sparsely furnished space. I wondered how people ended up here. Suddenly, I noticed a large hand print glowing on the wall. Fear soaked my gut. *I couldn't move. I couldn't sleep.* The green hand gripped my thoughts for the next six hours.

In the morning I joined the other ladies in the dining hall (I didn't mention I might be going crazy.) I wanted to get to know them better. We had only spent a few hours visiting in a common living area the night before. The women were absolutely lovely and all so different. Mary* had a job, a home and a longtime boyfriend until he shoved a gun to her face. He told her he'd kill her if she didn't leave. Mary boarded a bus and found herself at a homeless shelter in Harlingen, Texas. I was reporting on special assignment.

The shelter closed its doors during business hours to encourage Mary and the others to go out and search for employment. After breakfast, the photojournalist and I followed a woman named Julie to a nearby warehouse. She was eager to check on her pet parakeet.

The shelter didn't allow pets and the warehouse owner graciously offered to tend to the bird. We spent a few minutes watching her fawn over her beloved before our next stop at the thrift store.

Julie reported for duty. We documented. I asked her why she volunteered. She told me she wanted to *feel needed*. I seemed to carry her shame around all day. *How worthless she must have felt?*

I'd known the feeling as a little girl. I balanced on wooden beams surrounding a playground at my newest elementary school (my third.) I focused on the beam trying to look busy. I didn't want anyone to notice me all alone *or maybe I wanted just one person to notice me and make me feel welcome.*

One impeccably dressed grandmother moved into the shelter because her son no longer had room for her. During the day she wandered around the grocery store. She'd never been homeless and she didn't have anywhere else to go. *I loved her earrings.* Some people made their way to a homeless camp in a wooded area by train tracks near the city's downtown.

I met a convicted murderer and his girlfriend living under the trees. He told me he had work construction but didn't want to leave her. His girlfriend suffered from bipolar disorder and he worried for her safety. In the woods people used drugs and alcohol. I watched an old lady sniff gold paint out of a water bottle. *Those folks didn't sleep at the shelter.* They didn't like the rules. The couple made a makeshift home with tarps and coffins (actually, wooden storage containers used to ship fancy coffins). Their home was dank but tidy. Oddly enough, the couple made their bed each morning.

Some of the men gathered and smoked cigarettes in the park. It felt like a car club or a fraternity. The guys, young and old, all knew each other. I was surprised to learn some of the men even had jobs during the day.

Others hung out near or at the library. We hiked to all the homeless hot spots before lunchtime. I was hungry but determined to live on a dollar a day like the others. I also ditched my makeup only to realize other guests still managed to put on a little rouge in the communal bathroom at the shelter.

The day brought loneliness, isolation and most unexpectedly *boredom*. I wanted a meal, a nap or a drink to pass the time. Ironically, many people told me drinking (and addiction in general) not only contributed to them becoming homeless but it was the reason they *stayed* homeless. Mental illness, medical or financial problems also topped the list. I don't remember seeing anyone holding a sign—advertising their condition. The people I met wanted to disappear. Business owners didn't want then around. Everywhere we walked I could *feel* the stares. Over and over I heard about bad breaks and the mental paralysis that followed. Some people lost their jobs. Others blamed traumatic events like the terrorist attacks on September 11th 2001.

Moving beyond trauma means moving beyond fear; a lesson I learned while body surfing in Santa Cruz, California as a girl. A wave whipped me around and I swallowed water. I started crying the moment I made it to shore.

I remember my father grabbed my arm and marched me back to the gates of the pacific. "You're going to get back in right now or you will be too scared to swim again."

Maybe he was right. I recall him sounding like a mad man as he tossed me out to sea. A veteran I met on the streets told me he just couldn't move past his trauma and defeat. *He didn't have the courage to start over again.*

Homelessness happens to other people. That's the judgment I rode into the shelter on. I never understood how deleterious judgments like this can be. *Judgments divide. Judgments define. Judgments make us feel safe and separate from the randomness of fate.* Sophomore year in high school my judgments made me turn down a date with a nice and cute guy because he didn't have a plan for college. I also steered clear of a lonely classmate rumored to possess a hit list.

Staying away and withholding kindness didn't make me any safer—I don't think someone with a real sense of belonging shoots up a school or mall. One kind act might have changed the life of a lonely teen. One date might have bolstered a nice cute guy's self-esteem (who has things all figured out, anyway?) And now I *know* homelessness can happen to anyone. Sometimes my judgments saddled me with an inferiority complex. If I deemed someone as better educated, better experienced or better dressed somehow I was lacking. I could have lived inside walls built entirely of judgments. That would have been just fine *except I wanted my world to change.* I wanted deeper friendships and better relationships. Sadly, I sometimes still catch myself making judgments like when I noticed a young mom wearing a revealing shirt. I stopped myself. Mother Theresa said "the more you judge, the less you love." Another lesson I hope Brandon learns early.

Fear is the paper on which every judgment is drafted. I know how griping it can be. I couldn't sleep the second night in the shelter either—the green hand warded off much needed slumber. The next day I gathered the courage to ask about the mystery hand on the wall.

The shelter director laughed. He told me it was a handprint left by a painter. The natural oils, trapped between the first and second coats of white paint, absorbed light and glowed (touché, universe.) *More proof we're all connected. More proof we leave our mark everywhere we go whether we mean to or not.* If only I'd been brave enough to find out sooner—I might have spread more kindness along the way.
*not her real name
(Disclaimer: Fear is an important human response. For more information read *The Gift of Fear* by Gavin De Becker. If an immediate sense of danger manifests physically DO NOT discount it. I've interviewed thousands of people and I've only felt this lightning fast impulse once or twice. I responded accordingly in those instances.)

Reporter's Notepad:

How has fear clouded your judgements in the past?

How can you make the world a better place by relinquishing those judgements?

Chapter 14: Learning from My Losses

"It's failure that gives you the proper perspective on success." - Ellen DeGeneres

A cascade of confetti signaled my defeat. I felt like a toy soldier grasping the ends of a smile like a falling parachute. I couldn't hold on. Tears fell with the paper rainbow as cameras pushed-in for my reaction (morning TV). I wore my disappointment and a California State University Fullerton T-shirt. The winner of the 2006 KTLA College Audition jubilantly clung to her oversized check worth $25,000 dollars. I wanted to be happy for her but I wanted to win more.

The lure of legitimacy sparkled in the spotlight. Deep understanding would one day pull the pin on this dream like a grenade (although, I wasn't there yet.) In this moment, I heard Micheala Pereia empathize. *She knew* how it felt to come in second. I don't know if she or if any of the other judges said it *exactly* but I heard "keep going."

I was born in Rantoul, Illinois in October of 1982. My parents lived in a trailer home near the now defunct Chanute Air Force Base (enough time has passed that my mom can laugh about the red and black shag carpeting and everything else.) My dad joined the military and my parents married shortly after my mother found out she was pregnant.

Days after my birth my grandfather took a private plane to fly his teenage daughter and her new little family home to Tulsa, Oklahoma. After the trip my father drove us out west to Beale Air Force Base in Northern California.

The trip proved too much for my mother's recovering body. She spent more than a week in the hospital with a serious infection when she arrived in California.

The Golden State felt pretty dark I am sure. My Abuela (my dad's mother) spent days trying to coax me into drinking from a bottle. I was less than a month old.

My parents never made me feel as if they regretted their choices. Yet, I often wondered what they might have found if they'd picked a different path. Maybe my mom would have been a great writer? Maybe my dad would have engineered airplanes? I unconsciously set out to prove they'd chosen correctly. I wanted them to think they were holding the million dollar suitcase on the game show *Deal or No Deal*. Every setback, every loss, every B minus made me question my value. (First born, what can I say?) In the fourth grade I anchored a school-wide broadcast. Younger kids knew my name and I felt important. I decided that's what I would do for a living. My parents would be able to take their little prize to the bank.

My plan was working. I leveraged the Audition loss into my first reporting job (I tried to forget the failure and the confetti.) I worked side by side with some amazing standouts. I found the extraordinary in everyday stories. I tried to play the role like a golfer aiming to improve my own game without concern for the other competitors on the greens. The talented people I've worked do this.

They're able to walk into a newsroom as if it's a grocery store with list in hand. They focus on what they need and move on. They're only concern is what's in their cart, not anyone else's.

Reporters who meander around the aisles and worry about what other people are buying don't go far. It takes drive, sacrifice (long hours, time away from family) and continuous professional development on and off the clock.

It really is a lifestyle. I accepted all of this for a while (blindly unaware of what motivated me). My compulsion to make my parents proud occluded my truth: my ambition was holding me hostage. I wanted the freedom to explore new opportunities and take time off to start a family. A phrase kept appearing over and over. Do I want to be right or do I want to be happy? Happy please.

Peace lives in the knowing that there is nothing to prove. This brings me to a full circle moment. One of my favorite college professors reached out a couple weeks back. We talked about the students eager to get into the TV news business, the industry and life in the real world. After we caught up she told me a poster from the Audition still hangs at the university. I smiled.

It's funny how things go. I've truly learned more from my losses than my wins. I don't know if my professor said it but I heard "keep going" (even dreams need space to evolve.) Oh, as for the winner. I was truly happy to see her on General Hospital not too long ago. The joy in my life gives me happiness to spare.

Plus, I know what it takes to keep striving for years. Sweet Michaela joined CNN—glad to see her come in first.

A former co-worker opened a bakery while two others landed jobs as correspondents. It was never about the gigantic glossy check for me or about the spotlight either.

Understanding what motivated me all those years allows me to redefine my notion of success. So far, my new working definition includes; family, balance, happiness, creativity and the knowledge that there's enough success to go around.

> Reporter's Notepad:
> What motivates you?
> What's your definition of success?
> What would you do if you didn't worry about pleasing or letting down your parents, partner or children?

Chapter 15: Connection

"We are like islands in the sea, separate on the surface but connected in the deep." -William James

I motioned for the on-call doctor to finish up his conversation. "It's *time*. I need to push." A nurse was helping him into an extra layer of clothing as if he were headed for the front row of Sea World's Shamu Show. His nonchalance made me feel like a pushy customer at a sushi counter. My husband counted eight to ten hospital staffers including an officious nursing student in our delivery room. Brandon clearly wasn't born alone and I sincerely hope he doesn't die alone either. My baby boy was born to connect, born to love, just like the rest of us. After his first cry and before his first meal he instinctively coiled his fingers around one of mine. At three months old he's developing more control over those little hands. He swats at toys, sucks on his knuckles and he still reaches out for connection.

Twice this week I unknowingly contacted friends who needed me. I brushed-off the strong urge to call them until I finally acquiesced. Too often I ignore these inner callings because they don't make sense or I am afraid I won't know what to say. I waited too long to call another friend after her father died. I sent a heartfelt text and told myself it was enough. I *should have* called or written or something. I never know what to say. By the time we actually spoke, she spent an hour comforting *me*. We talked about Brandon. We talked about the weather. We talked about her father's final days.

My friend flew a thousand miles to sit at her father's bedside. Not long after she arrived she instinctively reached for her father's hand.

Her young nephew saw this and asked what she was doing.

She told him "taking away the hurt." Sometime later, she left her father only to find her nephew stroking his hands in her place. "What are you doing?" she asked. He said in his little boy voice, "taking away the hurt."

I've witnessed unfathomable sorrow on the job. During the time I spent reporting I met families at their worst often interviewing family members of murder, drowning, fire, and accident victims. I've found sorrow thickens the air inside a home like mold. I remember standing with a weeping grandmother after she buried three grandchildren. Fire destroyed their mobile home. The youngest baby was just 15 days old—too young to even smile. I faced the absurdity, as a reporter, of asking why? Why did a baby die in a fire? The answer will never come.

Sometimes life sends only a mist or a drenching rain and sometimes softball sized hailstorms come our way. I've wambled, worked and walked through my own storms. I am a different person than the woman sweating in a hospital bed three months ago. I certainly see more sunny days than storms.

However, I don't want any impressionable twenty-five year olds to think nostalgia, melancholy or loneliness never creep it into my 7-day forecast. Even now, in the quiet of the morning or in the stillness of the afternoon, these emotions can move in swiftly like a tropical storm in Florida. A wise woman coined the phrase the "loneliness of motherhood."

Sometimes these feelings are masked as boredom or frustration. I consider them an alert. These emotions signal a profound need to *connect* either with a loved one, with myself or with a higher power.

(The universe is the ultimate social network.) Sometimes, I find it's a call for creativity. I started sharing my writing with the hope that my rough pieces might fit neatly inside someone else. I believe human creativity is rooted in a desire for connection.

You're not alone—these words take away the hurt. My friend's beloved father died on a Saturday. His wife, daughters, son and grandsons took turns holding his frail hands until his breath weakened and eventually stopped. *He didn't die alone. The world isn't cold, either*. He left his body in peace surrounded by people he loved. His departure reflects the power of 72 years of true connection. This is my hope for my son and *this is my hope for all us. Being there. Reaching out. Sharing hurts. Telling truths. Slowing Down. Choosing love. Seeking joy. Embracing vulnerability. Finding Humor. Staying connected.* That's all anyone can do (except for maybe my on-call doctor— he might want to pick up the pace).

Takeaway:

Connection is the bedrock of a life truly lived.

Chapter 16: Ode to My Ladies

"I awoke this morning with devout thanksgiving for my friends, the old and new."-Ralph Waldo Emerson

I can do big things with a bulb syringe. Call me the boogie gestapo. I spent all of Saturday evening and Sunday on patrol due to Brandon's first cold. Perhaps, I am a little overzealous when it comes to clean noses and nappies for that matter. "He's breathing fine. Let him be," my husband said at least once over the weekend. I squirted saline drops; I pulled out the Boogie Wipes® and the humidifier anyway.

Maintenance is critical especially now that I am a mother. I realized this months ago when I spotted two (okay three) hairs on my toes. *This never would have happened when I was single.* I decided right then and there I must maintain a good clean shave every single day. If I let it go, even for a day I'll need a machete and thirty minutes to deforest later. Heaven forbid the stars align and Brandon falls asleep, my husband and I are both awake and I'm swinging through the Amazon. *Maintenance.* This theory applies to the laundry landside and clutter catastrophe, just the same.

I've been striving to maintain a steady writing schedule too. Up to this point I am doing so-so. Although, I am pretty sure my work reveals at least three things about me readers wouldn't otherwise know. A.) I am either a tortured optimist or a recovering pessimist. B.) I have a secret obsession with all things British.

I just love the word nappy and mum. In college, during a trip across the pond I found myself in a little pub in SoHo. I pulled a Madonna and tested out my best English accent. A cute Londoner, in a caramel colored leather jacket, whispered "I knew you were from the states the whole time" after my lovely flat mates blew my cover and made me blush. They shouted "you're American" from across the bar. I am certainly too busy for pubs now but I'll make time for the Duchess of Cambridge any day of the week. How would Prince George feel about a play date? Well, as they say in the old country: 'the sun never sets on a mum's work.' That is the expression, right?

C.) Lastly, I may not be wealthy but I am rich with friendships.

On television, online and at work women too often either judge or disparage each other. Why else would we watch the Real Housewives? I feel female friendship should be celebrated. It is an absolute necessity in our lives. My husband is my best friend but out of respect for our gender differences I give him the twitter version of everything. The best thing I can do for our marriage is to "Be Calm and Shave On." My girlfriends near and far cheer me on. They validate me in ways no man could.

Its empathy and camaraderie I need as a mother. Friendship also takes work. Don't call for a few weeks/months/years and I need two hours to catch up. Sadly, this means the call is less likely to happen (text messages here, a tweet there, maybe a Birthday card).

Sometimes it's the best I can do. A girlfriend recently posted that a "Like" on Facebook is a virtual high five. Love it! High fives all around!

The phone is not my favorite form of communication yet it's a must for me. At this hour, I am involved in a multi-player game of phone tag spanning several states. Maintenance. I fall short far too often, but I keep trying because I love my friends like I love fish-n-chips, Duchess Kate and Adele.

> *Takeaway:*
>
> *Maintenance is much easier than playing catchup. Do your best to keep up, especially when it comes to life's most precious gifts!*

Chapter 17: Tunnel Vision

"I wanted a perfect ending. Now I've learned, the hard way, that some poems don't rhyme, and some stories don't have a clear beginning, middle, and end. Life is about not knowing, having to change, taking the moment and making the best of it, without knowing what's going to happen next. Delicious Ambiguity." - Gilda Radner

    Darkness stretched toward the center of my script from all four corners of the television screen. My knees locked. My cheeks blushed. I kept reading as long as possible. Eventually, I started babbling as a confused teleprompter operator scrolled in vain. 17 seconds. That's how long it took everyone in the control room to recover and take me off the air. My *pride* took a whole lot longer. Thankfully, a graphic covered the screen during my inadvertent/live Darth Vader impersonation. I can't remember who caught me before I hit the newsroom floor. I do remember awkwardly laughing off my temporary aphasia and praying the air check would mysteriously disappear.

    I've fainted several times in my life. I realize that's quite a lot for someone born after 1920. The first fainting spell happened at the roller rink in the fifth grade. "Look guys I can skate backwards! Oh...no..." Twelve seconds after my fall I found myself belly up with a ring of partygoers surrounding me. "Yes, I am okay. Anyone still think I am cool enough to couple skate?"

    The next time it happened on the side of my house. I fell and bruised my tailbone during an intense game of tag with my brothers around our home.

I fainted when I pierced my belly button in high school. I *nearly* fainted several times during pregnancy with Brandon, which I learned is a common symptom.

Fortunately, I knew to look out for the tingly sensation, dizziness and tunnel vision. I felt a familiar sensation looking down on beach, buildings and blue gulf waters on my thirtieth birthday. My insides tingled. Fortunately, I wasn't about to faint this time around. I was about to jump out of an airplane.

Sky-diving seemed like the perfect metaphor. I would leap into this new decade with gusto. I didn't fear the experience. Although, I did enjoy swapping hyperbolic text messages with a friend before our impending jump. "I can't believe were doing this! I am soo nervous!" The instructor told me the free fall would only last 60 seconds. I tried to save any real dread for 90 seconds out. We boarded a tiny aircraft at the Brownsville airport on October 20th 2012. The pilot snagged the only seat.

The other three passengers and I hunkered down near a flapping door (something about a busted latch). I actually think our odds of survival spiked the second we jumped. The plane made me nervous. During the descent I felt an odd sense of peace; a stillness while traveling at 9.8 m/s/s. I told myself, "This will only last a minute. I must try to live in this space of uncertainty." I clenched my eyes and breathed in the unknown. It felt like I was traveling sideways through a tunnel. Soon the parachute opened right along with my eyes. I felt a rush of cool air and adrenaline.

Gratitude filled the next six minutes before we landed on a soft sandy patch at South Padre Island. I've gone through many tunnels in my life.

Heck, my twenties felt like one tunnel after another. What's going to happen? Will I figure it all out? Will my parachute open? Will I ever find my footing? Inside the tunnel I have a tendency to overshare and ask for advice. What should I be doing with my life? If only I had allowed some space in my life for uncertainty. Uncertainty makes things exciting. Uncertainty leaves room for blinding clarity in hindsight.

Less than a year after my soft landing, a pretty nurse told a group of expectant mothers, "When the pain feels unbearable just remember it's almost over." The sky-diving experience taught me not to spend too much time worrying about actually giving birth. It *would* happen and I *would* either survive or I wouldn't. The nurse was right. When I felt as if I couldn't handle any more pain (sans epidural) my son barged into the light and took his first beautiful breath. He survived *his* first tunnel too.

Everyone goes through these spaces of uncertainty. Entire industries do the same. During a lunch with a reporter friend we talked about the future of TV news. "What's the industry even going to look like?" She asked. Over sandwiches and ice cold water I contemplated the question. Will everyone drop their cable subscription and use a smart TV connected directly to the internet? Will we all pick and choose the stories we want to watch? Will local news get stronger? Will *only* network news survive? Will we connect to hyper-niche websites to get the news?

Questions often grow inside a tunnel like germs in a petri dish. I've learned I can't get the answers until I *surrender* to not knowing.

Like the TV news industry, it turns out I am entering another tunnel and another tunnel isn't too far behind.

I wonder if my writing resonates with anyone. Am I making a difference in this world? Am I doing a good job as a mother? I must breathe in this space of uncertainty. I feel a familiar flutter; a dizzy, tingly sensation in my stomach—not going to faint this time. Along with excitement, uncertainty leaves room for great possibilities. I am feeling the buzz, the joy, the power of surrendering to those possibilities.

> Affirmation:
> I am learning to appreciate the excitement and rush of not knowing exactly what lies ahead. It's thrilling and makes my life more fun.

Chapter 18: Casting a Villain

"The search for a scapegoat is the easiest of all hunting expeditions."- Dwight D. Eisenhower

I fidgeted on a wooden pew in the middle of the Cathedral of the Annunciation in Stockton, California. Sunlight beckoned beyond stained glass until these words sliced through my boredom; "for God sees not as man sees, for man looks at the outward appearance, but the LORD looks at the heart." On this random Sunday (sometime between O.J. Simpson's joyride and the Spice Girls world tour) I made a resolution to see as God sees. I decided to look for beauty in everyone. Sometimes it was as simple as thinking she has "nice eyes" or he's got a "gorgeous complexion."

This generosity of spirit even extended into high school. I once stopped a gaggle of girls from egging prostitutes on Wilson Way. I felt *pretty* good about myself. That is until Sue Ann* entered the scene. I can't say I despised her. I will say I thought she stole my boyfriend. Amongst my friends I called her something particularly offensive in 2000—let's just say it's used in a garden. She wore kinky curls and a Marilyn Monroe inspired piercing above her lip. We shared a Spanish class and nothing else (or so I thought).

Everything from her style to her voice irritated me. Immaturity guided by insecurity made me truly believe she was some kind of villain. In truth, we were simply teenage girls sifting through our own hormones and heartbreaks.

It's no wonder I encountered a villain on my quest for Prince Charming. I grew up watching Disney movies.

Ursula. Maleficent. The evil Step-Mother and her delightful offspring. Fairytales may end "happily ever after" but they often start with an innocent young girl and the villain trying to ruin her life. Before we vilify the villains I must point out Maleficent only wanted an invitation to the party. Angelina Jolie played this up when she took on the role in the Disney flick in 2014. Ursula battled some serious body issues—like Chaka Khan trying to fit into Kate Moss' tentacles.

Divas don't shrink Ursula. Let's not forget, Cinderella's Step-Mother was left to raise three teenage girls on her own. Now, that's wicked. I encountered villains out in the field while reporting, too. Or perhaps I used the archetype to write better stories. Enter the avaricious tow- truck driver, or used car salesman, or roofer preying on poor old ladies. The world and the people living here are far more complex and as the internet meme goes "Be kind, for everyone you meet is fighting a hard battle."

In my real life, casting a villain made me a blind victim, unable to see anything beyond my own discontentment. I've fallen into this pattern enough times to sew an entire wardrobe. A beloved boss who called me mediocre became a villain. If only I could escape her wrath? My poor mother certainly got typecast.

(Yes, Mother *this is how* I am doing my hair.) I am not proud of the avalanche of self-pity Sue Ann* brought on either. After reading *If Life is a Game, These Are the Rules* by Cherie Carter-Scott, Ph.D. I realized (shocker) the problem starts and stops with me.

Rule number 7: Others are only mirrors of you. My boss, my mother, Sue Ann* and anyone else who's ever frustrated me only mirrors qualities about myself I don't like or qualities I want but feel I lack.

It's not enough to look for beauty and goodness in those I like. I need to look for beauty in *all—even those who drive me crazy.* The real work isn't turning the other cheek; it's looking in the mirror. I'll never see as God sees but I do better when I take my blinders off. The next time I spot a villain or feel outside frustration, I'll know it's time to look in the mirror and work on myself.
*not her real name

> Reporter's Notepad:
> Who are the villains in your life?
> Are there any ways you have cast yourself as a victim?
> How can you take more responsibility for your own behavior?

Chapter 19: Vision Boards and my Non-linear Life

"Life's too short to live someone else's." - Nathan W. Morris

In 2006, I scurried around the KTLA newsroom simultaneously trying to blend in *and* get noticed. I pulled tape, ran errands, wrote scripts and web stories. Watching the unsung heroes of the newsroom changed my perspective on life. Editors stay calm in the chaos. Editors transform shaky shots. Good editors act like Usain Bolt crossing a finishing line with 30 seconds to deadline. "The video is in!" They make reporters and producers sweat. A staff editor also made this lowly intern very grateful by cutting her demo reel. Tape to tape, no less! I paid a company $200 dollars to convert the Beta SX to VHS.

In those days, my professors still advised students to send out tapes. During my next job search I sent out DVDs (nearly a hundred during the height of the Great Recession.) Today, news directors expect links. *Flash frame: Somewhere between a dark edit bay and a labor and delivery room I started making vision boards.* Editing tape to tape takes patience and vision. Linear editing, as it's called, is like wrapping a Christmas present—you need precisely the right amount of video.

Fail to cover one second of voice track and poof you've got a black hole or a piece of irrelevant video (a flash frame). Old school editors did so in *real* time—if the video was two minutes it took two minutes. Non-linear editing, with a computer program, gives the editor freedom to experiment. Move clips around. Ctrl Z: undo.

Flash fram: On those vision boards, I cut out magazine images to represent the life I want. A little bit of this, a little bit of that. Hey, ho, hey ho...no one needs to know it's out of sequence. (I am not advocating this all you NPPA photographers—just sayin'.)

I've lived my life a little out of sequence. I left high school early in order to relocate when my dad's work demanded it. I didn't drop out per sé. I just opted to take the California Proficiency Exam instead of finishing all of my classes or starting at a new school. Classmates told me things wouldn't work out. That I would never go back to school. I would fail. I feared they were right.

I promptly started community college taking Radio/TV/Film classes and all the prerequisites I needed to transfer to a University. I graduated Cum Laude, a little late but I graduated. *Flash frame: in 2011, newly single, I created my most complete vision board with a typewriter, a baby and a ring.* During my internship I realized I shouldn't start my career in Los Angeles. On election night, KTLA led with a breaking news stinger announcing the Kevin Federline/Britney Spears divorce. Not real news.

I left Southern California in an overly packed Honda Civic a few months later. My belongings kept sliding and hitting the back of my head until I finally stopped in Texas. I didn't know how things would turn out but I held onto faith things would fall into place.

Flash frame: I got my last period a year ago just a few days before Christmas. Editors rarely pick the video they're asked to edit. Their job is to do their best arranging and rearranging, slowing down and speeding up the elements to create the best possible story.

I've lived everything from blue, shaky times to lovely happy years. I won't ever get the chance to go back in time and play basketball for Coach Modesto the year I left High School. I guess my life is more linear than I would hope.

I've moved past personal and professional failures like the caffeinated gum debacle—don't ask. Rhonda Bryne's **The Secret** led me to the conclusion that I am indeed the editor of this life. My vision. My best. Circumstances will change. I keep rearranging. *Flash frame: My husband and I weren't married when we found out about the baby— we were planning to get married down the line. The baby readjusted our timeline.* I can't take credit for the good things in my life but I can thank God or the Universe for listening. I can hardly believe I once expected life to unfold in the same way for everyone I knew. Go to college. Get a job. Buy a house. Blessings don't come one size fits all and neither do our challenges. I am learning to leave some things on the cutting room floor. I can't dread what may come and I am no longer dwelling on the past. I have enough faith in myself to deal with things as they come. Only this moment, please and thank you! *Flash frame: I've covered most of the empty spaces in my life I see fewer and fewer flashes of disappointment and doubt. My new vision isn't on a board. It's a banner of love, creativity and faith waving like a clear piece of video on the inside of my heart.*

Takeaway:

Throw out the timeline and outdated expectations for your life. Make a vision board of only the things you actually want, not the things you feel are expected or traditional. Remember: you have the right to write, re-write and edit your own happiness and it doesn't need to happen in any particular order.

Chapter 20: Milk, Cookies and the Selfie

"Taking care of yourself is the most powerful way to begin to take care of others." -Bryant McGill

Two chewy chocolate chip cookies rested coyly on a small plate my husband left on the kitchen table for me. I blissfully indulged. Of course this wasn't a quiet moment—I don't get many of those anymore. The sound of a Playtex breast pump cranked. Over milk and cookies I contemplated my new role and what it means to be a mother. Admittedly, I feel an epic shift to my sense of self. Obviously, there are physical changes. Some of my best bits now flip and flop. Seriously, I don't need a bra— I need a spatula.

The emotional changes are a little more difficult to pin. My needs don't matter as much as my son's needs but is it *okay* to have needs? Americans and *American women* especially obsess over the concept of self. The selfie made it into the dictionary for the love of Nancy Grace. Oxford not Urban—just to be clear. I know this because not only was this trending on Twitter but this "talker" made it to producer's rundowns from Spokane to Fort Meyers.

The history of the selfie doesn't exactly stretch back to a cave in Spain. Self-expression *is* something innately human. That's why folks start a Pinterest account, right? We want to know ourselves and we want the world to know us, too. Sadly my generation can take credit for the superficial selfie. As an older Millennial, I can tell you we used real cameras in the beginning. (Here's another bit of trivia, before twerking we called it grinding but let's get back to the slightly and sometimes overtly selfish selfie)

I've always felt a little vain and self-indulgent when I snap one. That's exactly what I needed to feel right now. Time to get reacquainted with myself. Hours after my cookies, I snapped a selfie just for me. I ran to the grocery store all by myself. I hate to admit it but it was the best 15 minutes of the day. I even wore my new scarf. I held a 'Keep Calm and Carry On' sign I keep in my car. I took this selfie to remind myself that *I matter*. I added it to my gallery already full of baby pictures. Before my little one made his debut I read *Scream Free Parenting* by Hal Runkel. The gist of his philosophy: in order to parent and love my son (AND I DO) I must take care of myself first. I had completely forgotten this little gem until I failed to eat or brush my teeth until noon on Tuesday (or was it Wednesday? The days blur together.)

The truth is I don't want to take time for *me* because selfishly I want to enjoy every snuggle and every smile. But my son needs *me*. He needs me to tend to him of course but he also needs the *me* that is more than a mother—the well-kept, motivated and happy me. I can't neglect myself without neglecting my son. This notion was reaffirmed while watching an episode of Oprah's Lifeclass on DVR. Dr. Phil told mothers everywhere "self-nurturing" is not the same thing as selfishness. *Word*. My self-worth is paramount. My son will learn the behavior I model. Got it. I am not saying I will always remember to take care of my needs first but I will try, for the love of my family. *I want to give them my best.*

> Affirmation:
> Becoming a mom, doesn't mean I'm no longer a woman. Taking care of myself is essential to caring for my family. Sometimes a little indulgence is a really good thing.

Chapter 21: ALL CAPS, SIDS and the Semi-colon in the Room

"Life shrinks or expands in proportion to one's courage." -Anais Nin

ON THE TELEPROMPTER, WORDS APPEAR IN ALL CAPS. IT'S EASIER TO READ AND THEREFORE EASIER TO ANNUNCIATE. SENTENCES SHOULD BE SHORT AND WRITTEN IN ACTIVE VOICE. (PUNCTUATION ALWAYS SEEMED OPTIONAL- SORRY PRODUCERS.) PERSONALLY, I WAS CRAZY ABOUT ELIPSES…AND QUESTION MARKS? *For some odd reason*. OVER TEXT MESSAGE, WRITING IN ALL CAPS IS LIKE SHOUTING. So, after a decade of SHOUTING it's no wonder I've forgotten so much of Grammar 101. Something I haven't forgotten? The lesson I learned in Señor Gallego's sophomore Spanish class more than 15 years ago. He told us "Your education is the sum of everything you learn, over your lifetime, subtracted by everything you forget." We'll it looks like I'm pretty much breaking even.

Watching the NEWS *at least* makes me feel informed. Although, more and more it seems like the same ten stories get rehashed on multiple platforms for days on end. As a new mom I should probably avoid this vicious news cycle for fear of getting trampled. Case in point; a horrifying story about SIDS or Sudden Infant Death Syndrome on the nightly news. An otherwise healthy six month old died unexplainably. WHY? WHY? WHY? Seriously, why does it happen? And why can't someone figure out how to stop it? The story TERRIFIED ME! PERIOD. EXCLAMATION POINT!

Lots of things terrify me lately; budgets, baby rashes, investments, cancer and don't forget punctuation. I am embracing Brené Brown's "Connection over perfection" model. If I allowed myself to fret over every word, sentence or semi-colon— I would never write anything. I should probably take a refresher course or pick-up an updated AP Style guide. *Agreed*. However, all the SHOULDS in my life often stack up against me, preventing me from seeing the COULDS and WOULDS. Perhaps, I am a little laissez fair about the placement of commas and capital letters. I must remind myself I am *not and will never be perfect.* PLUS, I AM NURSING AND TYPING AT THE SAME TIME. LOOK BABY, NO HANDS.

Okay **really**, really bad joke. I blame the hormones. Back to those pesky fears...Warren Buffet said during an interview on CBS 60 minutes "If you're batting a thousand than you're playing in the little leagues." I suppose someone other than my mom needs to read my work then. Gulp. Well, Señor Gallegos the good thing is: I haven't given up on my education! I *am* still learning. Thanks to Dr. Brown, Oprah and fellow writer Catia Hernandez Holm for inspiring this Aha: I can't live for the applause (a la Lady Gaga) nor die by the critic's sword. My goal is to put my thoughts and words out there and hopefully they'll make someone smile, or think, or better yet dream.

> Affirmation:
> I will continue to learn and grow for the simple enjoyment of learning and growing. I do not need to accomplish anything in order to validate the importance of those experiences.

Chapter 22: Lifelines, Deadlines & Million Dollar Dreams

"Know what you want to do, hold the thought firmly, and do every day what should be done, and every sunset will see you that much nearer the goal."
- Elbert Hubbard

It seems I traded the newsroom for the living room, when I started staying home with my son—more specifically I landed on the left side of the couch watching ABC's Shark Tank. Instead of dinner and drinks with friends, on Friday nights, I watch the parade of folks many of whom are mothers and fathers hawking goods on TV. Some of the ideas really are amazing. If you've seen the show...you know some are not. Most of the inventors need a lifeline, an inlet into an industry or an infusion of cash.

Hearing their stories oddly reminds me of one of my Aunts. She is always waiting on those elusive winning lotto numbers to fall into place in order to change her circumstances. You know the type. She's got a terrible case of "someday" or the "one of these days." She'll take that trip to Hawaii one of these days. Or she'll buy all of us houses on the same block, some day of course.

This evening I am sitting right smack in the middle of mommydom saying to myself one of these days I will... organize my closet/publish my book/start a book club...heck, read a book again for that matter. My best friend is anti-someday. She's the kind of gal who jets off to Peru even if no one wants to go along with her. I always felt like I was one of those women.

Now, I am not so sure. I devoted my twenties to chasing my dream of becoming a reporter. I always thought I would make it big (drum roll...) someday!

However, I wasn't just dreaming. I was doing. I started paying dues by taking a job in Midland, TX. I practically pulled my hair out.

Deadlines ruled my life for six years. I lived on adrenaline and thrived on feeling the frenetic energy of barley making my time slot. I also spent holidays away from family and scraped by financially. I fully understand how lucky I was to get the chance. This is by no means a complaint but certainly it wasn't easy. I heard 'no' far more often than I ever heard 'yes.' I went to work before dawn and ran from start to finish before I left my job in 2013. Instead of sprinting from the studio to the edit bay I am now running from the changing table to the washing machine.

Deadlines don't exist in my world anymore. In fact, my sense of time doesn't exist. Being at home with a newborn is like spending a night inside a casino in Las Vegas—there is something in the air that makes you lose track of all time. What? The Talk is on already? Pre-baby I wrote every single day. Now I can write anything I want and I find it hard to get motivated. Such is life. I suppose I used deadlines like a crutch, to get through the ho-hum days. I mistakenly thought I was disciplined.

Now, that I am a mom I need more discipline than ever. I keep asking myself who do I want to be in six months? Do I really need another piece of chocolate? I don't want to die in the groove on the left side of the couch nor do I want to give up all of my dreams.

I need a lifeline and really and truly would love an infusion of cash. Enter my brilliant idea for a super high tech baby product! (As *never* before seen on Shark Tank) I came up with this winner while dealing with one of my son's fussy periods, ironically at 4AM.

So my BF, the bawdy and ballsy one with a love of travel, tells me I should make a prototype. She also says I should write more and start a poetry website. The writing isn't paying bills but it does fill me up. Why do I run from it like it's a chore or worse a J-O-B? Once again, I ask myself who I want to be in six months, anyway. A lottery winner would be nice, although, I've already cashed-in on the relationship and mommy jackpot. I am certain this is someday. One of these days, I've arrived.

I can't wait for a better or brighter day I must pledge to continue dreaming, writing and creating. I will build my creativity and I will dig deeper and find the discipline it takes to continue to craft a good life. There is some good news— I've thrown out the timetable and thankfully I have a whole lot of lifelines I can call upon if I need them.

> Takeaway:
> Someday is a beach in Neverland, if you don't take action. Create a plan with small actionable steps if you really want to change your life.

Chapter 23: Write Tight

"The advice I like to give young artists, or really anybody who'll listen to me, is not to wait around for inspiration. Inspiration is for amateurs; the rest of us just show up and get to work. If you wait around for the clouds to part and a bolt of lightning to strike you in the brain, you are not going to make an awful lot of work. All the best ideas come out of the process; they come out of the work itself. Things occur to you. If you're sitting around trying to dream up a great art idea, you can sit there a long time before anything happens. But if you just get to work, something will occur to you and something else will occur to you and something else that you reject will push you in another direction. Inspiration is absolutely unnecessary and somehow deceptive. You feel like you need this great idea before you can get down to work, and I find that's almost never the case." — Chuck Close

An eighties model limousine pulled onto the California State University Fullerton campus. Before he stepped out of its green interior, I'd never heard of Stephen J. Cannell. The legendary Hollywood producer and writer (*The Rockford Files, 21 Jump Street* and *The 'A' Team* to name a few) gave a talk to hundreds of students. Cannell talked about love, life and mentioned only one secret for writing success; a plot twist in the second act of a story. His work ethic was the *real secret*. He worked in a furniture store by day and wrote for hours at night, *for years* before he ever sold a script, he told us.

    After the speech several other students and I were lucky enough to join Cannell for lunch. We took a ride in his limousine and learned about his life. He told us his wife was his best friend and even though he was a man in Hollywood he never betrayed her trust. He built a successful career but it didn't shield him from loss. His youngest son died during a beach accident—quick sand. His life sounded a bit like a movie. The experience was humbling. He inspired me to write whenever possible because anything really is possible if I decide to make it so.

    I rarely get writers block anymore. I rarely get writers block *if I actually sit down to write*. Before TV news I secretly enjoyed the promise of a blank page. I felt like a prize winning writer without a keystroke. I spent hours just thinking about how great my work could be, if ever I decided to write. I gave up this luxury when I started reporting. I didn't have time to luxuriate in the words. My veins pumped ice as I met excruciating deadlines, every single day. Sometimes I was writing ten minutes to air. Sometimes breaking news rattled an otherwise ready rundown. Sometimes I spent one commercial break texting a police chief only to type up the story the next break. "The turn and burn" of daily reporting made me thrifty and stingy with the words. I learned to write like a sculptor. I could see the end result and I chipped away until my vision emerged. Delete. That was the most important key on the board.

TV news writing gets a bad rap. Scripts get rehashed so many times Jimmy Kimmel makes a video mash-up every other week. TV news writing isn't all bad though. It changed how I write.

Mervin Block taught me "shorter, sharper stronger." Before TV news I tried way too hard. To steal another hella cool word from my youth in California, I wanted my work to be *tight* or amazing and exceptional. Now, I let the words flow and don't worry about anything but flow. Instead, I focus more attention on the edit, the re-edit, and the edit of the re-edit.

I still find the beginning of a story blocked by barricades, at times. Instead of wasting time I maneuver around the blockade to the middle or the end of a story and work backwards. I just begin wherever I can muster the inspiration. I've written tens of thousands of words in my lifetime. I've written by moonlight in the English countryside after imbibing on Absinthe (the drink Van Gogh was drinking when he cut off his ear.) I've written in the car and on top of live trucks. I've written on the beach and on planes. I've written in newsrooms and in my quiet apartment. I've written on my smartphone while my son sleeps. I've written for hours after work because that's the only time I could devote to writing. It worked for the late Stephen J. Cannell. His work ethic and genuine love of writing continues to inspire. He graciously shared the biggest secret of all—just start wherever you can and wherever you are. He was exceptional. I know I've got a long way to go to achieve my writing goals. However, I must simply sit down and begin. Thanks to TV news I can share one of my own writing tips: in order to write *tight*, one must write tight.

Takeaway:

In Television news there is a long held belief: it takes 10,000 hours on the air before a TV personality finally becomes truly comfortable. Get started wherever you, don't worry about your performance in the beginning. Simply commit to putting in the hours needed to hone your craft—whether it's baking, business, boxing or something entirely your own.

Chapter 24: Projectile Peas

"Don't worry that children never listen to you; worry that they are always watching you." –Robert Fulghum

Brandon started boycotting naps this week. He apparently hates peas. My eye hurts from too much typing and reading on my smart phone and I just want to eat a piece of cake. Correction: another piece of cake. I really need a walk after my fling with chocolate icing but my little one finally fell asleep. No go. I breathed deeply to avoid going berserk. I can only go forward.

I've noticed Brandon is increasingly fussy lately. He can't crawl. He can't sit up on his own and I see it in his eyes and hear it in his grunts—he's ready to move (I hear ya my love.) I am frustrated too. I am working on this compilation of lessons I hope to teach him. Somehow I've lost momentum. The devil knocked on my door and delivered a bouquet of freshly plucked doubts. Add three ill-timed nap-ending phone calls and curse words started going off in my head like a fireworks display.

I thought of an old photographer friend, a charming curmudgeon who happens to know a lot about life. He ranted every afternoon his phone sounded. "Don't they know I am on deadline?" Rick said every time he received a call. I always wondered why he didn't silence his phone. When my phone went off again and again I thought "Don't they know it took me two hours to get this baby to sleep two minutes ago?" Um...no they don't, shoulda turned off the ringer. *I can only control my own actions.*

Frustration is a function of life. My adult brain knows this but watching my son fuss and struggle on his mat sounds an alarm deep inside. I hear echoes of his frustration in my own.

I want to crawl for him. I even get down on the floor. This habit of trying to "fix" or help a situation appeared in my reporting too. When an interview subject took too long to answer or couldn't find the right words too often I filled the silence to ease my tension. The best answers usually dangle at the end of a long pause. I don't know why I had trouble waiting. I wanted to fill the space and wall out any and all frustration or embarrassment for the person I was interviewing and myself.

It's not guaranteed I will be around long enough to eliminate all of Brandon's frustrations in life. Plus, doing so can actually hurt him. Google brought me to an amazing article by Althea Solter, Ph.D. Solter writes babies must master new skills to build confidence. Her "Aware" parenting philosophy states "bouts of fussiness" typically precede mastery of things like crawling or walking.

Learning to eat solid foods is another skill. I strap Brandon into his high chair and with green spoon in hand I peddle peas. I personally only tolerate them. My mother once pretended to spit up spoiled split pea soup in our front yard. I stood outside in disgust. The sound of every splat killed any chance I'd one day enjoy peas. My mother laughed for days over the gag. As Brandon ate another green spoonful I saw the same disgust. "You don't like them?" He spit green puree far and wide. Nope.

I told my husband he didn't like them just as I predicted. Yet, I went to sleep wondering how much my facial expressions really shaped the exchange.

Every day I feel like I am in a nature vs. nurture showdown. He doesn't really like anything I've fed him so far. I probably project my own disgust onto this poor boy. I didn't eat peas during pregnancy maybe that's why he doesn't seem like them? Maybe I don't like being frustrated. Brandon is too young to like or dislike the feeling of frustration. He is just experiencing it. I must encourage him to keep trying without coloring frustration negatively. It's a function of growth not something to avoid. I wish I'd figured this out ten years ago.

Projections can be the pitfall of parenthood. I want Brandon to make his own decisions. He can't do that if I rescue him or tell him what to like or what to think by projecting my likes and dislikes onto him. He's a baby. Maybe one day he'll like peas. I need to encourage him to try new things, push through frustration to master new skills. I need to allow him to struggle. I need to own up to my own discomfort when it comes to feelings of frustration. In the same vein I must give Brandon the chance to dislike peas on his own. No more projecting, no more projectile peas (let's hope).

*Update: Brandon now loves peas and he can eat them all by themselves. I still hate them.

> **Breakout Extra:**
>
> My mother says "the most difficult part of motherhood is letting go of the dream you hold for your children and accepting they have their own dreams to fulfill."
>
> **Affirmation:**
>
> Struggle is a natural part of learning and life. By swooping in to rescue my son at every turn in order to make myself feel better I take away opportunities for him to use his imagination and I erode his ability to gain confidence.

The B-Block

Chapter 25: Need the loo, eh?

"How do you want to be remembered? As someone who did the best she could with the talent she had." - J.K. Rowling

    I've visited way too many public bathrooms in my lifetime. It's one of the least glamorous aspects of reporting. Sometimes a gas station loo was actually a luxury. During a major grass fire in Midland several years back I literally couldn't wait. The situation escalated. Flames grew in the distance. Smoke extended for miles. I danced by the tall grass and barbed wire fence. The heat radiated off of the dusty roadside. I didn't dare sip from a cold water bottle even though I so needed a drink. Weeds and mesquite dominated the West Texas horizon. Firefighters warned us to stay put for our safety. Emergency crews closed the interstate and blocked the roads we'd traveled. Two photographers and I couldn't get out let alone drive to a bathroom. So, between a news unit and a live truck—I peed (praying the firefighters didn't see).
    Names, phone numbers, quotes, poems, love notes, and the human trafficking hotline are all things I've noticed tagged on bathroom stalls. I found similar signs of life on the United States/Mexico border along the Rio Grande in Texas while working on special assignment in 2010. I found rosary beads and torn pages from a bible. I found notes and a phone number on crumpled up college ruled paper. Undocumented immigrants left traces of themselves even while trying to hide from the Border Patrol. It's remarkable how humans can use a bathroom stall or a tree on the river to whisper, "I was here."

In the summer after eighth grade I traveled across a different border into Victoria, British Colombia. A group of students and I lived on a sailboat for one glorious week. We saw killer whales and bald eagles. The trip opened my eyes to a different world. I knew things would improve beyond adolescence. The world was so big! Some of our Canadian tour guides taught us the phrase "eh" (This boat is amazing, eh?) I wanted to be the gal to bring this simple phrase to my high school in California. Silly, eh? I just wanted to impact my circle even in this miniscule way. The phrase didn't catch on but it taught me something about myself and human nature. I don't believe this desire to be remembered or noticed is something we learn. When I noticed Brandon roll over back to tummy for the first time his eyes shimmied around until he found mine. I smiled and he lit-up knowing I had witnessed his feat. He wanted me to see him. He wanted to make his presence known. "I am here, mommy," he said without a word.

    Carving a name onto an electrical pole or tagging street signs or bathroom walls seems to be one of the least evolved ways for someone to be remembered. The rest of us blog, paint, post, create and some of us raise children. We impact the world by teaching right from wrong. People leave behind traces of themselves by encouraging a friend or by fanning their creativity.

    I've visited quite a few bathrooms since leaving the business. Now, I check for diaper changing tables and watch for family restrooms.

    By the way, the best bathroom hands down belongs at the top of the Huntley Hotel in Santa Monica, California.

The glistening Pacific Ocean meets a mellow soft pink, blue or orange sky painting this breathtaking view completely anew each evening. The awe inspiring sight from inside the back stall lives in my memory even though I never left anything behind. I was here. I was here. I was here.

> Reporter's Notepad:
>
> What mark do you want to leave in this world?
>
> How do you plan to carve out your legacy?

Chapter 26: Poverty

"The wealth of a soul is measured by how much it can feel... its poverty by how little." - Sherrilyn Kenyon

My first winter in the Rio Grande Valley delivered one very cold snap. Temperatures in the 20's literally crippled the usually warm border region. Officials shut down roads, opened up shelters, and a bevy of reporters spread out from the citrus orchards to the impoverished colonias. The Texas Attorney General's office defines a colonia as a "substandard housing developments often found near or on the Texas/Mexico border where residents lack basic services such as drinking water, sewage treatment and paved roads." While covering the cold I found myself in the trenches of real and unbelievable poverty. I'd never seen such conditions. Orange extension cords tethered families and trailer homes in western Hidalgo County.

Electricity was a far scarcer commodity than a sense of community. Shivering children ran up to us in their pajamas, wearing shoes without socks. Cold air collided with heat from our news unit as we greeted them. Neighbors gathered. I wore a pair of borrowed teal gloves my news director graciously offered when she noticed I didn't have a pair. Winter was almost over and I didn't think I needed them. On Christmas I wore flip-flops. The year prior I covered the death of a homeless man who died in the elements in Odessa, TX some 13 hours north of the border region. I knew cold could kill but the RGV was the paradise many retirees go to escape the harsh winter months and to get cheap meds in Nuevo Progreso, Mexico.

The cold caught me off guard as it did the folks I met that day in 2010. The kids appeared cheerful at least. Their families swapped electricity and collective shock. Of course, no one could remember the temperature dipping below freezing especially during the day. The families I met needed many things but right now space heaters topped the list. Their homes were clearly too hot in the summer and far too cold in the winter. Plywood and not-so-much as of a sliver of insulation separated most of them from the outside.

    I noticed many dirt lawns and some dirt floors during my visits to the colonias during my time in the valley. It was life on the fringe like I would never have imagined. I snagged a few interviews and chatted with all the wide smiling little kids clenching their teeth gleefully, the way kids often do around a TV camera and a microphone. I felt guilty in my borrowed teal gloves. Just before I stepped into our heated SUV I gave them away. I would eventually buy my boss another pair. I couldn't just leave and I knew she'd understand. She once gave me something like $80 dollars to pay off a water bill of a woman I'd profiled. The elderly lady learned about a leaky pipe when her bill spiked. She stopped eating to pay it until a caregiver called us. My boss wasn't alone. I suspect the little old lady from Donna never paid another water bill.

    I witnessed real kindness after stories about children and the elderly. After my story aired during the cold spell, some moms from surrounding cities delivered socks and space heaters to some very grateful families. They couldn't imagine their own kids enduring such conditions.

I can't imagine watching Brandon suffer. Compared to the kids living in these impoverished sub-divisions he's ridiculously blessed.

He's got socks and toys galore. We even turned our spare room into a playroom and then back into a bedroom now that our little girl is on the way.

I've enjoyed watching him socialize with his friends as they've transformed from babies to toddlers. It's amusing. One boy picks up a book and the other grabs for it clumsily. "Mine," seems to be a concept Brandon knows instinctually. Sharing is something he'll learn in time. If I do my job right I hope.

The issue of poverty is complex and heart wrenching. Yet, I can't talk about the poverty I witnessed on the border without talking about the generosity. I found time and again the poorest people were quickest to share a smile or a meal or willing to string an orange extension cord if their neighbors needed it. Wouldn't our world be so much better off we all acted as lights in the world for our neighbors?

> **Takeaway:**
> A lack of resources is nothing compared to a lack of connection. Even families living in abject poverty can teach the importance of giving, sharing and community. Give a hug if it is all you can afford.

Chapter 27: My Default

"The trick is to enjoy life. Don't wish away your days, waiting for better ones ahead." -Marjorie Pay Hinckley

I pushed as Brandon looked out from his stroller. His eyes darted around curiously. Leaves swayed in the wind. I went over mental to-do list. I needed to pack, clean, write, do laundry, shop. "I just need to get through today, get through tomorrow and get through my flight on Thursday. Get through the drive on Friday. Get through the party on Saturday." I said to myself.

Get through. Get through. Get through. I can't just get through my life! That can't be the goal. I spent years waiting to get into the news business. After I finally landed a two year contract I wanted to get through every contract I signed thereafter. Reporter friends actually say "next year will be better because my contract will be up."

My walk ended and I never once took a deep breath. I didn't enjoy the breeze. I didn't enjoy the sunshine. I've gone years like this at different times in my life. It's a worn groove in my mind playing by default. I need to do better than just getting through. Chances are I will get through no matter what. I want to enjoy my life. I don't know why it's so hard for me. I packed. I wrote. I washed. I scratched things off my list all while attempting to savor my last few days with my husband. I reminded myself of the importance of living for the moment. I must relish these glorious days as a young family.

I guess it's just so easy to fall into the groove of everyday; breakfast, tummy-time, crying, nap-time, lunch, dinner, bath and collapse.

The days passed by and I made it to the airport. Brandon fell asleep and I looked around the crowded terminal. I spotted a familiar face. Former Los Angeles Mayor Antonio Villarragosa stood a few feet away. He wore an American flag pen snapped to his dark lapel. Something made me raise my hand. I waved and he walked over. I shook his hand and asked to take a picture. He told me his niece was attending my alma mater. When Brandon woke up they took a picture. He was cordial and kind. Life can be so interesting when I pay attention—when I look around and forget about getting through.

My plane landed in California. I savored three beautiful weeks enjoying my parents, my brothers, my nephews and my sister-in-law. The clock kept spinning, a Malaysian jet liner disappeared and my time with my first family ended. I returned home to my husband, grateful.

A week passed and Brandon turned six months old. I cried following his six-month doctor visit. During his bath that night he laughed and gave me a look as if acknowledging the passage of time. We're on an adventure. Where will we go, who will we meet? We're not getting through, it's just getting good. I must avoid hitting default button and enjoy these passing days.

> Affirmation:
> I chose the pace of my life. I don't need to run around with a pen in hand, crossing off my "todo" list every second of every day. I can decide to savor and linger in the moment.

Chapter 28: Our Vows

"It is not a lack of love, but a lack of friendship that makes unhappy marriages."
-Friedrich Nietzsche

Paper. That's what you give for first wedding anniversaries. That paper should not however contain a list of grievances. I learned this painfully in past relationships before I ever said "I do." I held things-in and let things go without mention until my love leaked out slowly like a nail in a tire. Eventually, the tire blew and I walked away. My list of grievances extended for miles.

In my marriage I vowed to speak up. I vowed to turn to my husband even when I wanted to turn away. In the last year I've wanted to avoid conversations. I've wanted to leave things alone after I woke up in the morning no longer upset about the thing I was upset about the night before. I couldn't and I wouldn't. *The vows.* I read them again the other day. We had them printed for our big one year celebration. I needed to read them again. I needed to remember the promises I made. I needed to be the open hearted woman who stood on a sandy beach pouring her heart out. It's so easy for me to close up—to choose negativity or to walk around in a fog.

Donald Steven Brooks, love of my life. I stand here today, in awe of the gifts God has given us. You are everything to me and I vow to always remember how lucky I feel this very moment. I vow to turn to you in moments of joy, loneliness, fear, frustration and boredom alike

I ask that you turn to me; I will share your burdens and champion your achievement. Only together, can weather the ups and downs of a lifetime of love. I vow to respect, honor and cherish you.
I vow to always try to make you laugh and to always give you the benefit of the doubt. I promise to encourage your happiness and success
I vow to stand by you in hard times too. I vow to give you time for Saturday Morning Soccer with the guys and time with friends.
I vow to nurture my own creativity and happiness—so we both bring more love home to share. I vow to listen. I vow to speak u. I vow to make your needs a priority. I vow to use kind words and to talk things out. I vow to be faithful in every way but most importantly in my heart. I vow to love you—more each and every day from this day forward.

Camaron,
I love you. You are my best friend. Today, I give myself to you in marriage. I promise to encourage and inspire you, to laugh with you and to comfort you in times of sorrow and struggle. I promise to love you unconditionally, in good times and in bad, when life seems easy and when It seems hard. When our love Is simple and when it is an effort. I promise to cherish you, respect you, to care and protect you but most of all hold you in the highest regard. These things I give to you today, and all the days of our life.
    I needed to read these words when I did. We we're budgeting and moving into our first house. It's was a thrilling time but all the stress caused me to stumble on the vows front.
    I promised to give my husband the benefit of the doubt. I promised to talk things out. I promised to turn to him for any and everything.

I vowed to nurture my own happiness. Marriage is an amazing covenant. I am greeted by the multitude of blessings it has bestowed on me each day. It's also a great reflection pond. I gaze upon my annoying traits, my weaknesses and my shortcomings as I gauge my reactions to my husband's actions. Too often I see selfishness in myself. I am stubborn and rigid. He is easy and relaxed. Before we married I read *Saving Your Marriage Before it Starts* by Les and Leslie Parrott.

The Parrott's talk about gender differences, expectations and healthy relationships. They say men need autonomy, quality time and to be admired. Women on the other hand need to be heard, respected and cherished. Don't we just want them to listen? I am so glad Donald is so easy to admire. He's a great dad and wonderful partner. His easy going nature calms me when I get too uptight or didn't get enough inner-beauty sleep.

I asked Donald what he'd learned in the first year of marriage about himself and about me. He said that life is better together *with me*. I asked him the same thing after our second year of marriage too. I love the dialogue and I continue to learn from his responses.

Life is better with him by my side most definitely. I just need to stay true to our vows. Love, speak up, listen and repeat.

> Reporter's Notepad:
> How do you stumble in love?
> Have you ever abandoned yourself in the name of love? If so, how?
> When do you turn away from your partner when you need to turn towards them? In anger? Sadness?

Chapter 29: Hollywood

"Real life is sometimes boring, rarely conclusive and boy, does the dialogue need work." - Sarah Rees Brennan

Brandon's puke smells like movie theater popcorn. More puke than popcorn but still there's a hint of butter. This is coming from a mother. My husband disagrees. However, this is 100 percent subjective and folds very nicely into what I am about to write. Please suspend your disbelief. Movie audiences have been doing so for more than a hundred years. I believe it's the contract ticketholders make. (Okay, there's a bomb on a bus and only one man can save the people onboard. I am with you, Keanu.)

I can't tell you how much I miss movies. I miss watching movies and trailers for new movies. Lately, my mode of entertainment is watching my little angel sleep. I feel guilty even complaining about what I've traded for this experience. It's like the first scene in *Pretty Woman*. "What's yo dream? Everybody's got a dream in Hollywood!" I am living my dream, not in a cloud or on a soundstage, but in the real world where every day creeps along full of chores and choices. I am pretty sure I am not the only mother to ever look down lovingly at their angelic babe only to see Jack Nicholson's wild eyed expression from *The Shinning*. Now that Brandon is a toddler he adds a crazed scream for good measure.

Parents are brave people. Allow me to use Jack Nicholson's filmography to explain. Sometimes I feel like the *One Who Flew Over The Coo Coos Nest*, *Something's Gotta Give* and really, *It's Complicated* (oh, wait that's Alec Baldwin.) Let's face it, there are only (dare I say) *A Few Good Men* left and I want Brandon to be one of them. Right now, raising a kind hearted kid and not a Menendez brother or mass murder is number one on *The Bucket List*.
Raising kids is problematic in our society.

The movie business, I so love, often glorifies violence and sex and downplays anything real. I am not here to bash Hollywood. In college, I loved a night out in Tinsel Town. I spotted a few celebrities out on the town and when I volunteered to fill seats during an award show for a cable network. However, I preferred meeting non-celebrities with big dreams. I met an up and coming actor at the very top of the Staples Center during a Los Angeles Lakers game. Jack Nicholson made an appearance at the game no doubt. The aspiring actor was so excited about his career it was inspiring. I loved hearing "I am an actor/producer/writer/whatever but I wait tables to pay the bills." There's nothing cooler than the bravery it takes to dream in the real world full of all those chores and choices.

I met a new mom at Target of all places and she's become one of my best friends. The first time we met up in 2014 we walked around OP Schnapel Park in San Antonio pushing strollers and talking about our dreams of becoming mothers versus the reality of how much work goes into it.

It's hard. And it is worth it. I am not the first to say it and I won't be the last.

I must keep that in mind when I am faced with more work than rewards.

Before my life ends, before I go to be with *The Departed*—I pray I do a good job at this motherhood thing.

My life is nothing like a movie. I am a long way from Sunset Boulevard. However, this is "*As Good As it Gets.*"

*Update: I've watched a full movie on Netflix since I wrote this Chapter and Brandon no longer spits up *now he throws food*. Lovely, right? Our little is already here! We're excited to welcome a son in 2017! Hollywood loves a good franchise.

> Takeaway:
>
> Don't expect a Hollywood ending, even in Hollywood. Life is FULL of chores and choices. The best choice you can make is to pursue your dreams and know that living them won't be any easier than chasing them.

Chapter 30: Glass Houses

"The family is the first essential cell of human society."- Pope John XXIII

Brandon's arms flailed as his screams intensified. His razor sharp nails caught my cheek. "You need to calm down," I said exhausted, frustrated and frazzled. Then a flash of understanding "No, mommy, *YOU* need to calm down." I've read enough self-help books to realize I'd fallen headfirst into my lower (limbic) brain as if it was an open manhole on the street. I needed to claw my way back to my higher thinking prefrontal cortex. I did. I hugged my crying baby and said "I don't know what you want but mommy's going to try to figure it out. Ok?"

I've covered far too many domestic abuse cases, during my reporter days. The usual scenarios played out; mothers hurting babies, daddies hurting mommies or caretakers hurting babies. I've ached right along with victim's families—a grandmother clinging to a flat photo of Austin, the grandson she'll never hold again. I've interviewed a woman who survived an attack only to learn her husband succeeded in killing her mother and three sons.

It's either all over the news or not covered at all. I happened to stop by a Mall in Modesto, California the year Laci Peterson went missing. I saw her beautiful face and pregnant belly on a flyer under my windshield wiper blade (before her body and unborn son's body were discovered).

These types of stories leave most people wondering how someone could do that to another human being.

It's my humble and non-clinical belief that these crimes are perpetrated by either a psychopath, (by all accounts Scott Peterson) the mentally ill or regular people who never learned how to deal with anger in healthy ways or worse never learned how to connect and love. Moral outrage won't cure a psycho or a crazy person. Moral outrage just shames all the regular people into keeping their struggles secret. I wonder how I can help strip away the stigma so mothers and fathers can get help before writing their own headlines.

In West Texas I interviewed a man—man enough to admit he had a problem. He entered a program called Project Adam. It focused on ending the cycle of abuse starting with the abuser. The man told me he knew he needed help after a relative was arrested for murdering his wife. He witnessed abuse at home as a child. The behavior carried over to his home as an adult. Ah, there's the rub. No matter our intention, it's difficult to escape the things we witness in childhood.

I was spanked exactly once. The punishment fit the crime. I slammed the door on my little brother. My father flipped. I'd run across one of his personal fault lines. The epicenter of his anger lived in his childhood. He couldn't undo the time he slammed a car door on my aunt's finger. The door sliced her tiny index finger. Doctors sewed part of it back on but she forever lost her nail. Her little nub served as a visual reminder not to slam doors. I did it anyway.

In high school I didn't just push my dad's buttons I smashed them with a sledge hammer. During one particular low I heaved his just made hoagie sandwich down our hallway.

This by no means justifies it but he was ranting about how I needed to be more aggressive during basketball games. *I'll show you aggressive.* I was 14 and hormonal. "Stop pressuring me!" I screamed. Perfectionists don't often do well with direction. I snagged the sandwich off my dad's plate and sent it soaring. Even I was shocked by my actions. I wasn't thinking.

No sooner did the meat and cheese hit the floor did my dad give me a heave-ho down the same hallway and rightfully so. After I landed in my room my dad walked away even taking my angry mother along with him and securing a suite in heaven, I am certain. It was a remarkable showing of restraint. He didn't know it but he was teaching and I was learning in that moment. He showed mercy and the respect I failed to show him. I don't remember the consequences that followed later. I remember his self-control and his unconditional love.

That's the thing about kids; they're built to test boundaries. Children learn by watching their parents' react to their behavior. I regret all the times my brother's and I tested my parents. I feel for those parents too weak to withstand the pressure—losing everything because they lost it for a moment.

Yelling is the two headed beast I want to keep out of my home. I've talked about it before. *Screamfree Parenting* by Hal Edward Runkel is my guide. Through the lens of parenthood I see my flaws reborn. I see how I'm going to have to work at not yelling. He's not even a teenager yet.

My son is already showing signs that he's not a morning person. Get ready for a raucous every time he's roused out of sleep. I can see the struggles already.

I've called my mom when he's crying and I just don't know what to do. I never want him to cry or hurt or make mistakes but he will. So, I talk about *how I feel*. I vent over ventis with friends at Starbucks whenever possible because motherhood isn't just magical it's maddening at times.

A young mother, close to me, shared a chilling story. While driving over a bridge with her two little crying kids in the backseat she thought about driving off and ending things for the three of them. Thankfully, she kept driving. Sometimes good people make devastating choices on an impulse. I think of little Austin in these moments. He died of blunt force trauma to his abdomen. I wept while reading his autopsy. I always cared a little too much as a reporter. I'll never know what led to his fatal beating. I just know he was once loved and somehow it wasn't enough to protect him.

I write these lines and think about Brandon. My intention isn't to gather stones to throw at homes torn by domestic violence. I want to start a conversation. I believe high schools should teach students how to identify their personal fault lines and how to recognize when the lower limbic brain is calling all the shots. America is only as strong as its weakest families (scoffing in disgust every time I see one of these stories won't solve the problem—not even if it's about Adrian Peterson).

I'll start first by making my own home the highest example of peace and love. I can only do this as a parent by expressing my own annoyance and anger in healthy ways. I am sure I will end up yelling at some point.

I've already fallen short. Every day is a chance to do better and to love more. Moms need other moms to share their feelings and find strategies to cope. I resolve to reach out to new parents to give them friendship, support and hope. Even as families spread out across the country for jobs and other opportunities, we haven't outgrown the need for a village to help raise kids. We all need the village and the village needs us.

> *Reporter's Notepad:*
>
> *What's your personal fault line?*
>
> *When do you find yourself overreacting most?*
>
> *What emotions come up when you feel yourself getting annoyed or angry?*

Chapter 31: Love Layers

"Courage is what it takes to standup and speak; courage is also what it takes to sit down and listen." – Winston Churchill

I clutched a stack of photos in one hand and shook the Police Chief's hand with the other. My body tensed. My thoughts narrowed like a ramming rod. I would get answers no matter what. He sat down hastily. He clearly didn't welcome this interview. He seethed with annoyance. I didn't care how he felt. He was going to answer my questions. A bitter, unproductive exchange ensued. The Chief at one point swiped the pictures before walking out of the interview to make copies. His anger startled me. By the end of it I was hammering back tears and wondering why he was such a jerk.

I left in a firestorm of disappointment. The photographer and I raced to the station. I expected the footage to explain the Chief's bizarre behavior. I wasn't prepared to see mine. What a jerk, I walked into the interview with my mind zipped like a freezer bag. I didn't listen. I didn't put my subject at ease. I locked out respect and I locked out my humanity. I watched the footage again with my news director. I needed clarity. I didn't say anything inappropriate. He was the one who stormed off but my delivery hit harder than his poor actions.

My news director called it. She said I wasn't genuine. I edged me out of the interview. She assured me my warm disposition could be an asset "there's nothing wrong with asking the murderer very sweetly 'where did you bury the body?'" She smiled and batted her beautiful blues for emphasis.

This is the hardest lesson I've yet to fully learn. My natural instinct is to close up, to get defensive. Now, when I feel myself shutting down I say to myself "love." It's a trigger to remind me to remain open. I don't have to like the person, I don't have to respect the person's behavior but I must show up ready to listen. Love needs to be a part of the equation. I am learning to embrace the definition of love as pure energy free from judgment and expectation. I try to view disagreements with my husband, as an opportunity to get closer.

If I question with love I don't need to direct the answer. I don't even need an answer. I just need to give the other person a chance to speak. I don't need to act tough because love gives me strength.
I watched Jenny McCarthy and Josh Elliot interview the creator of a website called seekingarrangement.com on The View. Two college co-eds sat alongside the creator and talked about the site and about getting paid for their companionship. McCarthy hauled in her judgments. Her questions pelleted them like paintballs. She didn't leave space for anything but the answers she expected. An unproductive, heated exchange ensued.

The whole thing reminded me of my own botched interview years earlier and run-ins in the newsroom. The interview was painful for me to watch. As a viewer I got nothing out of it but McCarthy's bias. I understood why she wouldn't let the girls off the hook. It did seem like prostitution to me too. I just wanted to hear *why* this was an option for the students in a space free from judgment. There was no love lost between McCarty and the co-ed from Drexel. Perhaps, the interview was one more reason McCarthy didn't last very long in her spot on the View.

It's still a struggle for me to bring love into every instance. Yet, the more inner work I do, the more I understand the entire universe. It's amazing. What's the 90's hit? Oh yeah, *"You Get What You Give."* No sooner do I remember to incorporate more love into my discussions and relationships, I see an article or an interview echoing the message. Looking back I learned all of this while body surfing in Santa Cruz, CA. Sometimes I listened to my instincts and rode the wave to shore and sometimes I dove through to avoid getting tossed around. Body surfing is an exercise in paying attention. One must listen to the wave and respond without trying to shape the outcome. I can't listen and respond without trusting myself. That's why I must know myself and *be myself* even when I am facing a powerful police chief. Listen and respond. Stay present in my own unique power and let love guide the way.

Affirmation:

I control my own thoughts and behavior. I chose a foundation of love and respect. I trust myself to handle any and every encounter.

Chapter 32: Move Fresh

"We keep moving forward, opening new doors, and doing new things, because we're curious and curiosity keeps leading us down new paths." Walt Disney

     A nightmare shook me by the shirt collar and rattled me to my core. I spent five whole seconds stunned. My fingers moved about the bed feverishly until I found my husband and baby sleeping contently. Comfort quickly crowded out the terror of not knowing where I was. Donald and I closed escrow on our first house. It is mid-May 2014. Brandon is crawling and so much happier now that he can finally move around. We've been living with my mother-in-law and I've been putting off baby proofing until we moved into our own home. I am so much happier knowing we will soon move into our own space. Who wants to be a housewife without a house, anyway?

My MIL is a widow and grateful for the company. I am grateful for her company and help with Brandon too. I left the world of TV news in 2013. More importantly I said goodbye to another batch of great friends and started over. The stress of moving *again* is overwhelming. I've moved something like 10 times in the last 10 years. It's time to settle-in. I'm tired of lugging around a "clean slate" and the compulsion to reinvent myself and the need to make new friends.

     I'm tired of unpacking dishes. I'm don't want to attend any more going-away parties, especially my own. My close friends and family live *everywhere but here* in San Antonio. Staying connected takes Herculean resolve. Sadly, I mostly rely on Facebook and increasingly infrequent texts and phone calls. I want to gather everyone up for some real face to face time (not on a device).

This is the life I chose. This is exactly where I want to be. I just wish I owned a private plane or a hot tub time machine. My nightmare disconnected me from time and space in the hollow darkness of night. Maybe someday I'll really be able to go back to my time in Long Beach or Midland. Then, I'd celebrate with a true and epic throwback Thursday. I'd go to a Rockhound's Game before skipping over to Belmont Shore for a Pepe salad with friends and family. I'd walk Pier 39 and Stockton's miracle mile. I'd eat In-and-Out Burger and ride the Pershing Rollercoaster before dinner. I'd skip pebbles on the Thames and stroll around the Getty Museum. I'd cuddle up watching *Friends* on a couch nestled on Woodduck Circle then I'd drop by Spalding Avenue in Fresno for a late night chat with my brothers.

Reporters live like gypsies—leaving everything behind with every new job. Every move and every stop shaped me while clearly shaving years off my life (I'm waking up in a cold sweat!) I can't start over anymore. *I never really did anyway.* I hauled around personal baggage, fears and expectations in a suitcase labeled new beginnings. I won't say it's my last move or the most important move I've ever made. *I already made that move.* I will say the best thing about my next move is that I will pack up my family and I won't go it alone.

Reporter's Notepad:

What big moves have you made in your life?

How did you reinvent yourself?

What baggage have you hauled around?

Chapter 33: Pixie Dust

"You receive from the world what you give to the world." –Oprah Winfrey

Shame gurgled at the sight of the almost empty black bin. "Ms. Brooks, we can offer you $2.45. We are going to pass on your other items because they're non-teen styles that don't sell well in our store." The hipster cashier managed to convey; you're old, out of touch and broke in 20 words or less. This was the second cashier to shove a bag of unwanted dresses my direction in the last hour. Each paid me a total of seven dollars while making me feel worthless in the exchange. Maybe, if I felt differently I would have spent the money on lottery tickets. Except, today I knew *I couldn't* win.

Money isn't just laced with cocaine and E.coli. For, me it's covered in "pixie dust." That's what one of my aunts dubbed the familial guilt. She always warns me to dust it off. This was the perfect moment for that sentiment. I walked out of the store with Brandon on my arm and two dollars and change rolled and wrinkled in my hand. Tears weren't far off.

Staying home with Brandon was a choice I made with little regard for finances. I knew the time with him would be priceless. I didn't mind giving up pedicures, daily Starbucks runs and Bi-weekly shopping outings. (Okay, I minded a little.) My husband makes great money and works hard but after health insurance, two car payments, diapers, hospital bills, food etc... We're like every other American family and back to broke. As my dad says about his own budget "were hemorrhaging money."

Since we moved into our modest house I've put a few grocery trips on the credit card as I've tried juggling startup costs and new expenses. The month was only half way spent and we'd spent almost everything. I didn't want to put yet another charge on our card. Instead, I yanked my best dresses out of the closet with optimism in my heart and baby on my hip. I would try to sell them at a resale shop to buy some essentials and feel better about our finances. Labels up for grabs: Rachel Roy, Calvin Klein, BCBG. The brands I stopped buying the moment I stopped working.

I've learned so much about life and so little about money in my 30+ years. I can't explain why it's so easy for me to spend for the moment rather than live in it. I feel inept when it comes to finance. My best friend berated me for not shopping around for a mortgage lender. We went to the guy our realtor suggested. He seemed fair and promised to push the loan for us. I still feared we would get rejected. The feeling mirrored how I felt as an 8 years old at a Walgreens. My aunt sent me in to buy pantyhose and I couldn't figure out the tax in my head. The cashier not so kindly nor quietly announced that I "didn't have enough money."

My family sent mixed messages about money all the time. My dad and his siblings were always "broke". My dad made a few bad business deals including a cattle purchase in the mid-90's that the family still chides him over. My mom however lived by the mantra that money "isn't everything" and "it comes and goes."

I adopted my mom's approach to money, probably because my Dad's left me feeling overwhelmed.

I told myself I didn't need to worry about money. I bank rolled my life on the notion that one day I'd pay everything off when I became a network reporter.

This boxed me into living for a dream I would outgrow. It also didn't hold me accountable to a budget. "If only I'd spent less than I made," I lamented at 28. It was then that I vowed to "get it together." I eventually read most of the *7 Stages of Money Maturity* by George Kinder. Clearly, I didn't fully get it. I did however pay off $10,000 dollars of debt I accrued while in a failing relationship and after a couple of big moves. I thought I'd learned something. I was wrong.

I still feel ashamed around money. I don't like to talk about it and I would rather avoid issues involving money. I still feel like a little girl without enough. I adopted my mother's philosophy but inherited my father's fears.

My dad didn't grow up rich. He was a first generation Mexican-American. His first language was Spanish. He put himself through college and then put my mother and then all three of his children through college. Expensive.

My mother didn't grow up poor. She attended private school and belonged to the country club as a girl but she is incredibly down to earth and disdains snobbery. She didn't worry about money until she started managing a home. After, more than three decades she's got it down. My parents have done well for themselves. Somehow, their feelings about money persist. My dad still says he's "broke— just on another level." My mom gives and gives and gives to all of her kids because "it's just money." She also spends, spends, spends even if it's in the name of a sale.

Modeling rational and intelligent ideas about money for Brandon means I need to start thinking about money rationally and intelligently. I'm just not there yet.

I can't say it. I must live it. That's the gauntlet known as parenting. I don't regret staying home all these months but when Brandon turned 10 months old started a part-time job at a non-profit. Financially, it was the best choice. It also gave me a sense of balance. of having a job and growing my career in a new direction. We will save and pay down debt and generally "get it together." Crazy as it may sound, we want to do this all over again sometime in the next couple of years. (We better start saving now.)

Update: It's been more than a year since I wrote these words. During my pregnancy with Addison I worked part-time with a non-profit. I've learned good and wonderful people can do great and wonderful things with their money. Reading *Living Well and Spending Less* by Ruth Soukup inspired me to improve my relationship with our finances. My husband doesn't worry. I am releasing my worries too. I feel confident about my financial future. I want my home and life to be filled with **more love than things**. She's inspired me to go on and the only way to get there is through planning, discipline and budget. I must also release the fears money unleashes in me. Over the years there was always just enough. Someday, *if I am open to it* I will find there's always *more than enough*.

> Reporter's Notepad:
> What's your relationship with money?
> How do you feel discussing money or paying bills?
>
> Affirmation:
> My relationship with money is evolving—money empowers me. Money I earn will be used for good in my life and the lives of others. I give and receive freely.

Chapter 34: It Could Be Worse

"At every step the child should be allowed to meet the real experience of life; the thorns should never be plucked from his roses." –Ellen Kay

News reporters can lean heavily on tired phrases. In a pinch (I couldn't resist) clichés can drive home (sorry) very relatable themes. In my experience one reigns supreme (okay, I'll stop.) "It could have been worse," trumps 'em all—especially, if a car has just careened into a house. It's the first thing people say after describing the boom.

My mind can cross the mental medium used to protect *what is* from some horrible and fictitious scene *possible* on the other side. I once thrived on this thinking. I read an entire book devoted to survival techniques in the early 2000's. If my eye ever pops out of its socket, I hope I can find a Dixie cup and some Duct Tape handy. Thank you Joshua Piven for writing the *Worst Case Scenario Handbook* Sadly, knowing things could be or could have been worse gives me solace. It's human nature.

I need not go further than the halls of my middle school to prove this truth. In 7th grade, unbeknownst to me my skirt wedged under my backpack for brief stretches throughout the day. At least I put my underwear on right side out (at least two days a week they end reversed). Even if it only mitigated my embarrassment by a smidgen, it was enough.

I think TV news needs and feeds off the premise "it could have been worse." Why else would TV stations air mug shots? In my dumpy mom clothes I can generally find at least one person looking worse starting at 4:30AM Monday-Friday. Hello face tattoos!

I've started trying to eliminate this extreme thinking. Bad things do happen but *so do good things*, every day. I focus on my relationship with what is. That's the only way I can improve or impact my life. It takes more practice as of late especially, since Brandon teeters around the couch like a drunken fraternity boy on a balcony. My mind starts firing. "Careful," I say with my lips and eyebrows rolled like a wet towel. I hope Brandon soon forgets these words. His bold spirit will serve him someday. I remind myself "persistence is a valuable trait," (Although, it is no less annoying in soon-to-be toddler form.)
I rationalize. He's going to fall. He's going to learn from each bonk. It is what it is I tell myself. It usually calms me down. Except, I wasn't ready to hear this story my husband proceeded to tell me.

    I was away at my new part-time job. My mother-in-law innocently placed Brandon on the hood of her car to adjust something (so the story goes.) She's 4'11". Somehow, my big boy shimmied to top of the white Toyota Camry parked on concrete floors in her garage. Donald said his precious little face bore a mischievous smile. He clapped his hands with glee. My mother-in-law couldn't reach him. Her friend (also, 4'11") ran to get my husband. I imagine the two Peruvian women with their arms outstretched in panic. All the while Brandon squealed with delight.

    I've watched my son crawl face first off of our bed so immediately my mind took the plunge. "He could have died or badly hurt himself." My husband laughed. He said the whole thing was hysterical. "I wish I had taken a picture." "Then you would have died" I said melodramatically. Seriously, he could have died.

I frequently kiss B's little head and thank the angels above. Really, I must focus on what is. He's ok, just a healthy, lively baby boy poised to give me a heartache and a headache at any moment. I love him and I can't keep him from climbing whatever mountain he chooses. I will probably say "careful" too often over the next 18 years but I am a mom and I am entitled. I don't need to but I'll say it to him as he grows up too. He'll just have to deal because— *it could be worse.*

> Takeaway:
>
> Focus your attention on dealing with the actual outcome not "what could have" happened. The worst does happen in some cases. Conserve your mental energy for trying times. Don't worry—just deal with things as they come.

Chapter 35: I must fuss

"Life is just a lot of everyday adventures." –Carol Ryrie Brink

    I yanked bobby pins out of a tangled twist with contempt. My attempt at a magazine inspired French up-do looked nothing like the perfectly undone look on the model. Tension corralled in my neck. My husband's silver Volkswagen taunted me from its parking spot. I was so hungry—I imagined I could make stir fry on the hood. The sporty coupe wouldn't start anyway. I left the lights on and of course my AAA membership expired two weeks earlier. A train screamed as I strained my voice trying to explain everything to my husband over the phone. Two days prior, I told him how much I hated driving his car. A truck blocked me into a space in a parking lot. I guess I looked ticked then too because one guy quickly told me he was moving it and said "there are no coincidences." Maybe not, maybe, I was just tired.

    That morning I wanted a coffee but the Jack in the Box was out of lids. I asked for iced-coffee. The drive-thru worker promptly told me they were out of ice. The machine either broke or some staffer used it all for the ALS ice bucket challenge. I'll never know. I was having THAT type of morning. I took some deep breaths. Twenty minutes and $160 dollars later a nice battery service tech handed me an iced cold bottled water. I relaxed and started thinking about regrets.

    I've heard it said that we only regret the things we don't do. I certainly wish I'd switched the lights off but regret seemed a little extreme.

    No, in my life I've only regretted my reactions, my own inaction and my own lack of preparation. Like in college when I passed up the chance to apprentice with a popular radio DJ in Fresno, CA.

I was already an intern and he asked me to stay on after my internship. I said "no." He used the word stoic in a casual conversation and I feared I wasn't smart enough to keep up. It took me two weeks before I looked up the word in a paper dictionary. We used those back then. I feel silly documenting my own blatant insecurity but I realize now that most 18-year-olds are full of them. Not knowing a definition should have been an invitation to learn, not a reason to retreat.

I'm coming to comprehend my own significance and insignificance. I know better than to allow myself to feel inferior now. Anything, I didn't know I could have learned. I regret not giving it a whirl. I was so worried so much about finding a relationship in my 20's. All that time could have been spent enjoying my freedom and time with friends. Marriage and family are beautiful gifts. My single life was too. (Traveling, pedicures, studying, late dinners and watching rom-coms whenever I wanted!)

The engine roared as the tech pressed the key. Paramour's "Ain't it Fun" shot out of the radio like a t-shirt from a potato gun. Irony hit me over the head. I finally left work and continued mulling over the last type of regret in my life; lack of preparation. If only I'd had more faith and actually prepared for the family life I wanted financially rather than fearing my own loneliness. (Onsies. Cost. Benjies.)

The notes of regret played in my head space giving me a chance to reflect. My best friend's mom once told me that when her husband died she missed fussing over his birthday dinner and cake. She didn't know what to do without him. I know I'll add more moments of regret to my list.

I can only commit to watching my reactions; choosing to act on opportunities, preparing for tomorrow and most importantly fussing over the people I love. I'll never regret kissing my husband the second I get home and playing with my son two seconds later (even if I am hungry and survived a not so stellar day). I must fuss. I must fuss over Brandon's first birthday in just a couple of months. I must fuss over my hair and over dinner with my husband. It won't always turn out the way I plan. I might end up with a stack of bobby pins and a headache but it's truly worth the fuss. One day I won't have anything to fuss over at all—I don't want to regret not getting gussied up for this beautiful, messy, unvarnished life. I will never know when I'll run out of chances to fuss.

Reporter's Notepad:

What regrets do you have in your own life?

How can you use those past mishaps to fuel a better future?

How do you fuss over the ones you love?

Chapter 36: Letter to me at 13

"Live simply, love generously, care deeply, speak kindly, leave the rest to God." –Ronald Reagan

Dear Camaron,

    Right now you're 13. You like movies, going to lunch with your aunts, drinking virgin strawberry daiquiris, writing, reading, playing outside, talking about boys and laughing with friends. You just celebrated your birthday with a great group of girls at Michael's Pizza. They invited you! You wore lime corduroy green paints and a matching blue and green sweater. Enjoy the breadsticks, the restaurant will one day go out of business and in a few days your grandfather will die. This is just a coincidence. It's not a sign that you're not meant to be happy or that your happiness precludes anyone else's. You didn't use up all the happiness in the world, there is plenty to go around.

    You're now in your thirties. You like movies (but you haven't gone to the theater since your son was born. Yes, you have a son! (So, stop worrying about the future.) You like going out to eat lunch with just about anyone, including your aunts and you drink virgin Daiquiris (you're still nursing.) You like reading, writing and walking outside and you still love talking about relationships and laughing with friends.

    Life is really good! Your parents are still married. Your brothers are all grown up. Cherish them. The loss of a dear friend in a few years will reaffirm this lesson. Smile more often. You look prettiest when you smile. Don't worry if your crush doesn't notice you. He may not even like girls at all. He'll become an actor in ABC movies and you will never run into him during your time in Los Angeles.

You will have a few more crushes along the way. Don't worry about them. When you grow up and meet your husband you will be glad nothing worked out with anyone else.

Also, in a few years if anyone ever asks you to "go see the stars" tell him it sounds nice, maybe someday, but not today-- otherwise you'll end up blurting out "now you have to marry me..." with the delta breeze blowing across the bed of a truck. He won't marry you. He will marry someone else. And you will too. So just say "maybe someday" instead. You're going to get your braces off, your body will change and you must know that you're enough as you are. Don't worry about what people think. *Worry about what you think.* You're so strong! You will love adulthood! The learning never stops and you will know so many great people you admire.

People will try to discourage you from pursing your dreams. Ignore them. It's more about their own insecurities than it is about you. Try not to dwell on the words of others. They'll forget what they said while you're still wondering what they meant 18 years later. It's just not worth it. Enjoy your life and don't try to understand everything. Understanding will come with time. The only victory in this world is happiness and peace. Pray for it and stay present!
Sincerely,
Cam

> Reporter's Notepad:
> What advice would you give yourself at 13?
> How would your life be different if you'd heard the advice?
> What are some of the things you loved doing at 13?

Chapter 37: Everything Must Go

"Anyone who has lost something they thought was theirs forever finally comes to realize that nothing really belongs to them." –Paulo Coelho

    We pulled up to Hearst Castle in our gold mini-van. It was 1990 something and I couldn't wait to walk the grounds and see all the belongings of notorious hoarder and newspaperman William Randolph Hearst. I'd read a biography about the mogul detailing his compulsion for things. According to the book (sorry can't remember the author) he tried to fill a lonely space created in childhood. As a teenager, I understood the power of things. I just *needed* a Tiffany & Co. bracelet and a Dooney & Burke purse (to be cool of course).
    My mother, brothers and some childhood friends and I marched room to room taking in the light. The place was full of regal things and a dearth of life. Sadness was set like a stone in the colossal California mansion's walls. Although, Hearst's things outlived him I imagine flood, fire or earthquake shall one day swallow up that old treasure chest. In this world everything must go. Nothing lasts forever.
    I've lost many things in my life. The waters off the Gulf of Mexico swiped a pair of sunglasses three summers ago. I lost an oval shaped opal ring my Abuela gave me. I keep wishing that one day I'll find it. *Don't get me started on cell phones.*
    I've lost and dropped my fair share. I fished one out of the toilet once or twice. Two years ago while pregnant I washed the sheets and my new HTC one.

The most disappointing part about the whole thing was losing my contacts. I moved to San Antonio only a few weeks prior to the phone baptism. I couldn't text all the friends I was thinking about. It cut me off from a world I once knew. My contact list still hasn't recovered. Perhaps, the universe was telling me to let go but I wasn't ready.

All the gurus at Harpo Studios, all the monks in Tibet and Christy Turlington will say "it's not the things but the attachment to things that causes suffering." I've stood with many people of all different ethnicities and ages in a wilderness of loss—homes burned, flooded or torn down by winds. I've walked blackened hallways, ashes at my feet. I've gazed upon withered ceiling fan blades sagging like a captive killer whale's fins. I've stood inside a kitchen flood waters up to my ankles. I'll forever remember the terrifying smell of burned plastic. Most people cry and tremble in disbelief. Surprisingly, many disaster victims welcomed me into their world. I arrived to document. I often felt like I was there to console instead. Some people chuckle at the randomness of what's left behind after a disaster.

I keep an aluminum trinket destroyed during a 75 thousand acre grassfire in New Mexico. A family returned from a trip to find nearly everything gone. They gave me the melted metal to remind of the devastation. I sometimes hold that token of trouble in order to remember the world is in flux. Nothing is permanent.

Right now, my husband and I are fixing up our first home. I won't be able to fill it with world class treasures like old Billy Hearst but everything inside will be ours. That's scary. I know what can go wrong.

I know fire, flood and storms happen. I know they can happen to us. The reporter in me wants all new smoke and carbon monoxide detectors and a home warranty. I really want security and a guarantee that nothing bad will ever happen. I could certainly allow myself to overdose on fear. Instead I try to focus on the flurry of gratitude I witnessed after every disaster I ever reported on. Families just like mine lost their homes but didn't lose faith.

I never enjoyed seeing families in this kind of despair but marveled at their resiliency. I felt privileged to walk in the wake of such heartbreak because hope and gratitude rush in to fill the empty space. People who lose everything are almost in a daze. They're grateful to be alive. Grateful their children are alive. They're grateful for they're families. The shock settles and gratitude permeates. The loss hurts just a little less because of it. Sometimes families don't survive. Every survival story warrants gratitude.

I remember one particular family in South Texas. A grandmother was raising her grandchildren and one of the little boys was about turn 5 (as I recall). They were living in one of the poorest counties in the United States and their home burned down. The boy's family couldn't afford to rebuild and so they were living on what was left of the porch when the photographer and I pulled up. Viewers saw the story and donated money for a hotel stay. I visited the hotel and found the little boy had more birthday cakes than he could eat and more toys than he could play with. He was so excited! I was too. Only pure gratitude can fill the gap between wishing for a different outcome and finding hope for a reinvented future.

Even after all I know and all I've seen I can't always shake my attachments to things or the past. Take that old gold mini-van for example.

I hated it when my parents bought it. Then I saw it parked outside of my parent's house during a nostalgic Google maps search in the newsroom a few years ago. It was a lonely early morning search. I was homesick and wanted to hop a flight. The search took me back and greeted me with a memory. This morning I checked again and the van was gone. How fitting. Goodbye gold van. Goodbye 90's. Goodbye childhood. In time everything must go. The only guarantee—gratitude will get me through whatever comes my way.

Takeaway:

Things won't make you truly happy. Love and enjoy the beautiful things you own—just remember one day you'll leave it all behind.

Chapter 38: Dumb Love

"You know you're in love when you can't fall asleep because reality is finally better than your dreams." – Dr. Seuss

Before I met Donald I was a hapless romantic. I once sent iced water flying across a wobbly table on a date. *Andy leapt from his seat, a wet spot shaped like Texas on his jeans. My face matched the red napkins. "Sorry I talk with my hands" (more so when I am nervous). I really liked him. I didn't even question the fact that he preferred spotting my dad while weight lifting at the gym to chatting me up on the treadmill. I also didn't wonder why he wanted me to meet his mother after only a week of dating. I've never admitted this to anyone before. I serenaded him by voice mail. A.) I am not a singer. Brandon actually screams "no, no" when I try to sing to him. That's a confidence boost when a toddler doesn't even like your singing. B.) I am not a singer. C.) I sang Mr. Big "to be with you" (before I discovered Carrie and her Mr. Big.) I was a fool. We had listened to the song while making out at his fraternity house. I am cringing as I reminisce. Dumb. Dumb. Dumb. I found meaning in the song. I thought he did too. Andy might have preferred a show tune. I am pretty sure he came out a few years later. Guess I wasn't the little girl for him. Oh, well I wish him the best.

This stupidity stretched back to middle school. My first boyfriend and I were goofing around at lunch. My drink spilled on him as he tried to tickle my waist. He made a very big deal about it. As a red flag waived I worried all through 5th period.

What if he didn't like me anymore? Distraught, I borrowed a dollar and bought a soda, rushing to his next classroom during break. As other kids filled the halls I stood like John Cusack in *Say Anything.* Except it wasn't a boom box.

I held up a Sprite and proceeded to dump it on my head while saying "I am sorry." Cold, wet and embarrassed I watched as he just walked away. I took a math test with sticky hair and a bruised heart and ego. That guy dumped me a week later. Good for him! This stunt deserved a lesson. *There is such a thing as too nice.*

About five years later on a date with a radio DJ I was that girl again. His car stalled. The Volkswagen Beatle needed a push to start. Mr. DJ didn't trust me with the clutch. Instead he told me to get out and push. Here I am 18 years old pushing a 6'4" 240 pound 30 year old as snug as he could be in his old bug. Older and wiser, I refused a second date. I didn't realize the first date was a date until we were the only people going to the concert, anyway. I've dated a tattoo artist, a photographer (dating a co-worker is a bad idea) the grandson of some guy who allegedly won an Oscar. I never got the chance to fact check. My family quite liked the idea of a chiropractor I was seeing in college. Free adjustments, I suppose.

He liked the idea of me getting fake boobs. Um pass. Upon turning 28 I kept thinking the same thought. I spent so much time trying to find someone; I should have been trying to find myself. It took another year and a bad breakup for me to wise up fully.

A friend sped up the process. While complaining about all the things my ex didn't do to make me happy this sage friend said "but that's not his fault. Your happiness is your responsibility." Life. Changing. How could I have been so dumb? Why did I think a man could make me happy? Who knows? I am still figuring it out but the years of dating debacles prepared me for the love I know now. Chiefly, the love I show myself.

P.S. This dating mantra: eased dating anxiety "with the right person I can't say or do the wrong thing." When I first started dating Donald I got my heel caught in my jeans and tripped. He caught me. Years of practice allowed me to tap into a reserve of self-respect once unavailable. I didn't apologize, I didn't get embarrassed. My cheeks remained a normal hue. I smiled laughed it off and held on tight. Here we go. The right man *shows* me in big and little ways all the time. Now, I must continue to show myself love and in turn I'm able show my wonderful husband the love he deserves. After all, he is the only man who's ever been strong enough to catch me when I fall.

Affirmation:

My nurture my own happiness so I can love more deeply. I don't need love, I chose love.

Chapter 39: Do you really think so?

"Failure isn't falling down but failing to get up" - Chinese Proverb

If my ego needs a good lashing; I sing karaoke, try on swimsuits or submit my work for review. Rejection excoriates the ego and that's a good thing. I am learning it's a layer of myself I need to pull back, if I want to grow and thrive. I've heard it said that the ego wants more; when the heart is grateful.
Just the other day, I submitted a piece of writing for a flash fiction challenge. I'd never heard of one but I wanted in (2014 is the year to put myself out there).The prompt: kissing. Here's what I wrote:

> *The Measure of a Marriage*
> *Divorce ended with a kiss. It was a bitter, rigid and final exchange. Two people parted after kissing for twenty-three years. The kisses almost never meant anything. Sometimes their lips didn't even meet. He often pecked her cheek before leaving for work. Those little kisses kept her quiet when she should have screamed. Angry words gave her lips the look of two tight ropes. His lips dared not dance across. She nagged he complained. Sometimes his lips tasted of alcohol or boredom. She hated the words he didn't speak. You're stunning. He never said that.*

Their lips became the measure of their marriage. He lost track, giving thousands of throw away kisses, years passed with little connection. In the early days, their lips rolled open and lingered sweet and moist like a delicious French pastry. They played a wildly relaxed game of double- Dutch. Their tongues knowingly jumped in and out at just the right intervals. Young lips so soft and pliable. Their first kiss happened on a park bench during an intermural soccer match. He broke away from the huddle to pitch the perfect smooch. She twirled right after like a girl, her arms as wide as her heart. Love she thought. Finally.

She waited for him to open her up day after day. Her lips grew tired and worn—bouts of loneliness shriveled her pout. The last time those frigid lips felt feeling she kissed the foreheads of their babies to check for fever. Those babies were grown and she wanted to feel again. This isn't love she thought. Always.

Her wedding dress was crème colored vintage lace. She wore her hair down. His tux shimmered under the ballroom lights. He slicked his hair back like James Bond. Stunning he whispered to himself as she walked towards him. The moment made him tear up and he watched the next hour pass in a blur of love. Then a pure, soft and loving embrace. Cheers and whistles serenaded them as their lips met. A kiss started a marriage.

As a newlywed I am curious about marriage and particularly how to keep our love buoyant as the years pass. I love my husband so much it's hard to think that our love will ever wane. However, I am sure it will. I want to pour so much of that love into every kiss when he leaves for the day. But some days those kisses are throwaways. I am busy fixing Brandon's breakfast or I am still in bed. This idea inspired me. I wondered if those daily kisses can become the barometer of a happy couple. I wanted this piece to say "pay attention to what's right in front of you." Good or bad I liked the message and the words I wrote. It turned out the judges of the flash challenge didn't think it was the right fit for their online digizine. It probably wasn't. Marriage is hardly cutting edge.

My ego shed a sad smiley faced emoticon and I felt rejected for a moment reading the email. I didn't let it linger. It's like dating, when I was still single not everyone wanted to go on a second date with me. That's okay. I tweeted "when I feel the sting of rejection I smile because I know my heart is pointed in the right direction." I've encountered a ton of rejection in my life. It took a whole year and nearly a hundred DVD's before I landed my second job in TV news back in 2009. I believe it takes a high tolerance for rejection and hard work to find big success in life. Sometimes I cower away from rejection. Other times I embrace it. Those are the times when I've found success.

The world is full of overnight success stories. That used to make me question myself in my 20's. When would I get my big break? I've learned it's never a big break.

In my experience little opportunities add up over time and hard work pays interest. The overnight success stories are a mirage.

That's why it's important for me to remind my son (who will one day read this) the majority of people who make a name for themselves strive and endure their share of rejection. My mantra during my DVD slinging days: *it's not a matter of if but when*. Rejection is a message reminding me to; work harder, get better, or keep looking.

This rejection also opened my eyes to another lesson I needed to learn. If the flash challenge judges had actually wanted to include my work in an upcoming literary magazine I would have thought "really, me?" I find the ego can play coy when someone says "I really like your work." It's the "really, do you think so?" disease. A friend tells me to keep up the good work "you're on the right track." I eviscerate my own confidence by responding "do you really think so?" This behavior is almost more harmful than stewing over a rejection.

I can't lean on someone else's approval for validation just like I can't collapse under the weight of someone else's rejection. I feel like this is a theme in my writing. I've written similar lines while preparing this collection of lessons for Brandon.

This is one of many areas where I still need to grow. I know letting my ego lead either reactions weakens my strength as a writer and a human being.

I want readers to enjoy and connect with my words. If they don't, no big deal, someone else might. My own approval is what matters most and that's got nothing to do with the needy ego. I need purpose not validation (sweet, a breakthrough!) I can thank Gary Zukav, author of the *Seat of the Soul* for nudging me along.

> **Reporter's Notepad:**
> How do you shrink or expand based on criticism or accolades?
> Do you feel you need validation?

Chapter 40: High, Low

"Life has its ups and downs. When you are up, enjoy the scenery. When you are down, touch the soul of your being and feel the beauty." –Debasish Mridha

Each day, at a certain hour, an empty sort of restlessness announces itself. The feeling begs for coffee, a walk, chocolate or good conversation and in years past more than a couple drinks. I never understood this feeling and often yielded to its demands to avoid any real self-discovery. I was too busy during the week, as a working reporter, to feed this hunger with alcohol although, every few months I found a sober driver and loaded up. I binged, often going months between bouts. Then at 29 I blacked out. I made a fool of myself in front of my now husband and I ruined a dear friend's sweater.

The details are all secondhand so I will leave them out. I remember waking up in a fog of humiliation minutes before midnight on a Sunday in December. A group of friends spent the evening at a dive bar called Jackie O's. I woke up alone and naked. My dress looked like a pink puddle on the floor and I felt like survived a storm. Donald left, like the gentleman he is, hours earlier (while I still had my clothes on). I figured I'd never see him again. I sent out a cheeky text message about feeling 19 not 29. Full disclosure I worked the morning shift and only ate a tuna fish sandwich for lunch eight hours prior to imbibing on kamikaze shots.

I wish I could tell you the prayer I prayed. I don't remember. I decided if I wanted a family and a new life I needed to start acting like it. No more sporadic binges.

No more feeling sorry for myself or my lack of genuine direction. I haven't over indulged since. And I am so much happier.

Yet, around 2 o'clock some days I can feel the pull. Low tide. I sometimes feel helpless, useless, bored, or lonely. My rugged shoreline, usually submerged by glistening water is exposed. Wedged between the activities of the day and dinner is this witching hour. I used to run out and grab a coffee and sometimes I still do. Sometimes I reach for a cookie and feel ashamed not too long after.

Sometimes I don't do anything and look around. That's the best. I breathe and acknowledge this powerful time. My emotional low tide reminds me that I have more work to be done. Dreams unanswered. More soul to find. More love to understand. More me to satisfy. I go outside or read to Brandon. I catch my son smiling and time passes. The routine rushes along. I sip my coffee or just indulge in a deep breath and feel comforted by this feeling now. I know it's the moment calling.

I must be present. I must be here, right where I am. Soon it's time to make dinner and pleasant sounds of grease popping in a pan. Garlic fills the air. High tide follows. Donald walks through the door. Brandon swells with excitement. I can't explain why the metaphor helps me. Maybe it's my love affair with the ocean or the fact I am so far away from a beach. I just feel so contented knowing the water always returns to the shore. Low tide doesn't last very long. By the time I make it to bed I am exhausted and grateful.

> Reporter's Notepad:
> Do you deal with highs and lows in your everyday life?
> How do you deal with your emotions when you're at a low point?
> Do you find clarity in these low moments?

Chapter 41: Not the end of the World

"What a country." –Rick Stewart

"Sometimes, I pity you!" Rick said as he shook Donald's hand for the first time.
"Rick!" I scolded as Donald chuckled confusedly. Rick and I doled out a few more handshakes before we left the city event together in a dingy unmarked news unit. Cigarette ashes clung to the dashboard as I clung to my self-esteem. "Am I really that bad?" I remember asking rhetorically. Rick shrugged in a navy blue news-issued tee, worn jeans and scuffed boots. Blonde hair looked neat and trimmed minus a rat tail at the back. The hue of his skin resembled the rusty red of an old caliche road. I knew his story. I knew way too much not to take this personally. Years on the road together made us more than colleagues. He was my older work husband and sometimes I hated him. We sat in silence as I seethed most of the ride back to the station.
I recalled that anger seared silence during a recent fight with Donald. I'd become increasingly irritable about our finances and new roles as parents. I suppose Donald finally understood Rick's pity.
"I am just trying to keep your aura or whatever it is going on with you from breaking me down." Donald spoke from several feet away. His body language kept me at bay. Awareness hit me like a puff of smoke. Okay, I really can be that bad!
Another bad memory floated to the surface like a dead fish. During a family camping trip almost 20 years earlier I woke up to a sleep walking six-year-old peeing on my head.

I shoved my little brother to the ground and started screaming. My teenage sized anger filled our campground.

In the here and now, I consulted google and promptly cleansed my aura based on a random Youtube tutorial. I felt better, kinda. I couldn't get over my husband's words. He needed to protect himself from *my bad energy*. I intended only to give goodness. Yet, my mother, father, brothers and friends know I am capable of less. I've raged over hunger, lack of sleep, frustration, boredom and sometimes I pity anyone on the soft end of my sharpened gaze.

This arguably justified flare up infuriated my mother back at the campgrounds. "It's not the end of the world, Camaron!" She shouted from another tent. "Grab some quarters. Go take a shower!"

Urine dripped from my scalp as I continued to shred through quiet and my mother's purse. I was pissed (pun intended) and quite frankly everyone needed to hear about it.

I would like to think I've matured since that night at the campsite or out on the streets with Rick. Perhaps, no longer being a melodramatic teen isn't enough if I still broadcast my animosity if only subtly. The fight with Donald forced me to focus on the energy I bring into our home.

Sometimes I can be lovely and loving. I need to work on the moments when I am not. I can't go through life making the people I love feel as if they need to guard themselves against my moodiness.

I think the pressure to be perfect can infuse anxiety and negativity into the everyday moments if I let it. This fight of course, isn't the end of the world.

I will probably need to meditate and cleanse my aura at least once a day for the next 50 years. I know I won't be perfect but I can surly I can smile more and keep my good energy in check.

> Affirmation:
>
> Good, positive energy impacts my life and family in good and positive ways. I choose to exude the highest level of peaceful energy *even* in moments of stress and frustration.

Chapter 42: No Youtube for You

"If evolution really works, how come mothers only have two hands?" – Milton Berle

Three F-words sum up the grunt work of motherhood; flexibility, follow-through and fatigue. I tapped my right foot with another f-word (frustration) the first time I wrote those lines. I didn't finish and failed to save the draft properly. The words vanished like sunlight at the end of a long day. Up until 5 minutes ago I couldn't remember the last word. I spent a week trying to remember, so I might start again. Then I laid down, my arm sore from the flu shot I accepted at Brandon's 12 month wellness check. The nurse gave my poor baby...ahem... My poor toddler five shots. I noticed a little leftover blue frosting in his ear. I pointed it out during the exam and the doctor called it a sign of a good birthday party!

Brandon especially liked the part where everybody sang to him. The planning consumed me. Everything carnival. Churros. Pretzels. Popcorn. Too much. Too much. So determined to finish a slide show of pictures I barked at my husband unnecessarily. I can be so rigid at times. I see the same relentless edge in Brandon. Our doctor said he acted like an 18-month-old as he attempted to snatch her stethoscope. She listened to his beautiful and willful heart anyway. He started acting like a toddler months ago. *I don't know why the birthday sent my emotions soaring like a Ferris wheel.* The up and down feeling made me dizzy. I felt like this ride just started. I am not ready to say goodbye to the baby I met 366 days ago.

Brandon taught me big love. He taught me how to live life. He taught me flexibility, not just with my schedule but with my expectations. I never wanted Brandon to watch TV. "No you tube for you" I often thought as I watched other moms and dads hand their children cell phones during dinner. My little boy ended up watching more TV than I hoped and less than I need to worry about. TV news also taught me flexibility. Rundowns must change with the news of the day. Babies demand the same dexterity. No nap- no write. No sleep-no groceries. Newscasts and diaper changes keep coming. You're only as good as your last one. Flow with the go!

Follow- through turned out to be the easiest mothering concept to understand and the most difficult to carry out. Following through and documenting my first year of motherhood, tested my will. I didn't always like my reactions. I don't know why I thought motherhood would make me any less human. Maybe, because I fancy my own mother a superhero. Brandon's mum still needs work.
The inner work I continue today mirrors the outer work Brandon must do. He's learning how to fall and get back up. He's learning how to speak and how to listen. He's learning to find joy in a slice of watermelon or blades of grass pressed between his chubby fingers. Sharing, giving, loving; I am continually humbled by the lessons.

The sleepless nights blurred together like lights at a carnival at dusk. Late night music helped. Brandon loves the Beatles. Meeting other moms to chat helped. Brandon likes checking out his friend's toys. Watching the time zip past gave me a chance to embrace the precious time we shared. The sleep deprivation doesn't last forever.

Audio books helped me stay connected to my old life. I can't always read but I *can* listen. Dr. Daniel J. Siegel and Tina Payne Bryson define good mental health as floating relaxed and happily down a river. The outer banks of that river represent the extremes of chaos and rigidity. Chaos is the out of control feeling I get when I can't get things done. Example: the slide show. Rigidity is the feeling I get when I tenaciously decide I will get things done at all costs.

In order to float the river like a happy person Siegel says to steer clear of either bank. No chaos and no rigidity for me. Brilliant. This explanation makes sense. In order for me to teach Brandon how to go tubing down the El Rio Feliz I must teach him how to express his feelings. Of course, this requires me to express *my feelings.*

The first year passed with purpose and naturally, I bumped up against the banks of chaos and rigidity from time to time. Yet, I feel so much joy in my heart for the journey still ahead. I learned that the price of every freshly minted moment is a gradual unrecognizable goodbye. The thrills, milestones and farewells amortized over Brandon's first 12 months and now my baby is gone. He turned into a toddler slowly and swiftly as night bows out graciously for the sun. This is how life retains value. Every moment really does matter.

It's a new day here in the Brooks household. We're on a different ride and floating a new patch of river. I am grateful for what I've learned and mostly how I've loved. My heart grew with all the hellos and goodbyes tucked furtively into each day.

Update: Brandon is not just walking he's running and growing into a very independent boy. On this evening he has an elevated temperature and is sleeping as I edit this page.

Naturally, I assume it is West Nile Virus. Some things never change, eh? I just love him so much. I can't believe how lucky *I am* to be his mother and how much patience it takes to be good at it.

Motherhood really is the biggest challenge of my life. Every time I am away from Brandon even for a few hours I see him again and tell him how much I missed him. He now gives big hugs, feeds his Thomas the train engine popsicles. He prays. He holds out his hand and reminds his father and me to be grateful for the simple things. We're so rich with the joys of everyday giggles. The sound of a bubble lawn mower melts my heart. My aunt told me it would be hard to let go of the different stages but "all of their little phases are so much fun." It's true. We're enjoying the daily reveal of his lovely personality.

> *Takeaway:*
>
> When your parents were kids they probably didn't even wear seatbelts. It's time to relax and give yourself a break. If a child ends up watching TV but learns to say please and thank you most of the time—you're doing just fine!

Chapter 43: Emotional Credit Score

"I do believe we're all connected. I do believe in positive energy. I do believe in the power of prayer. I do believe in putting good out into the world. And I believe in taking care of each other." –Harvey Fierstein

    I gazed at the empty space between my fingers. I needed clarity and decided to take an adult education course entitled "Strengthening Your Intuition." The instructor Sonia Beatrice a psychic/healer told us the exercise could take some time. We needed to be open minded. I'd never seen or thought about auras much until recently. My husband called my aura to my attention during a marital squabble. He's not one to talk about auras or anything supernatural. So I took notice. He thought I needed cleansing. Earlier in the year a man claimed to see my mother's aura too. It was a weird coincidence I wanted to explore further. My mom told me the whole thing shook her up. I am also a firm believer in the power of intuition or instincts. I was riveted when I read the book *Blink: The Power of Thinking Without Thinking* by Malcolm Caldwell. Caldwell gave some amazing examples of research done to understand this realm. He even described the work of researchers learning about body language indicative of divorce. The seeds of divorce start with something as simple as an eye roll.
    Ms. Beatrice started the class by talking about "emotional credit scores." She said low emotional credit scores correlated with depression, negativity and illness. Higher scores resonated with happiness, health and well-being (Doesn't that make sense I thought?)

     She led a guided meditation to help us collectively elevate our scores. The room felt lighter and brighter. Was this the power of suggestion or something bigger? I will never know for sure. The experience reminded me of the uneasiness I felt when I walked into certain courtrooms, homes or even while walking a cell block in a county jail. Sometimes the people I met while reporting left me feeling discontented, drained, or sad. Inversely, some people can just lighten the mood and lift up my spirits.

     Ms. Beatrice said it was important to cleanse, meditate or pray to protect my energy from the outside influence of others—just as water warms ice cubes those same cubes transfer cool energy to the surrounding water. Marriage and motherhood hold me accountable to my moods. I can't disappear into an all-day nap or blow our monthly budget on a Target run just because I feel a little angst. I must monitor my emotional credit score like I watch what I eat or how I spend. My intention isn't to obsess. My intention must be to be better for the love of my family. I must also keep good company. Speak positively and try to burn bad energy on a walk or in a yoga class. Sometimes I must turn to a good friend to help me vent.

     In the tiny classroom, I kept my hands outstretched for a few moments longer as the brisk fall air crept in to cool the classroom from an open window. More than a year had passed since I started reflecting on life as a new mom and all the emotions I encountered.

A glimmer of pink and orange blurred around the outer-edge of my fingertips. I can't say for sure if I saw my aura or my eyes blurred just enough to make my skin appear to spread out beyond the natural boundaries. It doesn't really matter. Trusting my instincts, living in peace and love isn't automatic. It turns out my emotional credit score; much like my real credit score needs constant monitoring.

> Takeaway:
>
> Mind your emotional credit score by taking time to do what helps you relax. Just like missing a car, mortgage or credit card payment can hurt your actual credit score; skipping a meal, missing a mediation session or just your morning walk can send your score plummeting.

Chapter 44: Determination

"He that can have patience can have what he will." – Benjamin Franklin

I met Hector as he lie in a hospital bed surrounded by friends and family. I timidly walked in to talk with him after interviewing his father. Bandages covered his chest and his hair was dyed. He wouldn't be competing in the upcoming swimming competition in Andrews, TX like he planned. Doctors doubted he'd compete again. *He almost died*. A fence pole impaled him in the wake of a bad car accident. He fell asleep at the wheel after a long day of school and practice. The distance separating his lungs and heart from a cold metal pole was bind-bogglingly close, tighter than any race he'd won I'd venture to say. Just a hair one way or the other and I'd have a different story to tell.

I told Hector I would be waiting for the call next year to interview him when he started swimming and diving again. I meant what I said but I simply didn't believe it was possible. I wanted to believe. I just didn't. The school year ended and a new year started. Hector endured lots of surgeries. I went about my daily reporting until the next fall I got the call. I couldn't believe it! Hector was back on the diving board. I begged my news director to let me go. He relented. This was a feature story for sure. It was one I thought the viewers needed to see.

Hector's dad said every dive pained his son. The rotation of his shoulder ached. The scar-tissue bound up his movements yet he dove anyway.

He didn't complain and really didn't have too much to say as I interviewed him at practice.

I told him if you end up going to state I will be there. I meant what I said but I didn't believe it was possible. Every. Single. Dive. Hurt.

Determination isn't just a muscle. It's a mindset. I've never flexed my determination like Hector Roman. The shy teen demonstrated what it means to persevere. Reporting gave me access to some amazing people.

I met Shilo Harris one year after an improvised explosive device nearly killed him in Iraq. He and his wife exemplified the power of human strength and love. Shilo was burned on so much of his body he agonized in a medically induced coma for months. Even through his darkest days Shilo retained his sense of humor. He told me the blast sent his helmet flying and the straps ripped off his ears in the process. His wife gave him a pair of fake ears—he kept in a box with his damaged dog tags and other momentos. When I met Shilo he had great aspirations. He wanted to meet President George W. Bush. He later sent me a picture of that meeting. He wrote a book about his experiences *Steel Will: My Journey through Hell to Be the Man I was meant to Be.* I've lost touch with Shilo over the years but whatever he's doing I know he's focused on what he gained in the blast, not what he lost. I feel honored to know him and to have shared his story.

I want Brandon to learn the value of determination—to never, ever give up. I've mistakenly believed in my own life from time to time that determination trumps patience. Patience uplifts determination.

Determination is nothing without patience. They're like really good teammates.

I've been writing when I can and I am determined to bind all of the lessons I've learned while reporting into a simple e-book.

This book is for Brandon and for me! It's a promise I made to myself. The effort reaffirms my individuality and identity beyond motherhood. I want to remind myself and teach my son how important it is to follow your heart and do your best. As a little girl I spent hours digging up a flashy piece of quartz crystal buried in the hard dirt in the California foothills. I spotted the treasure while hiking. I used sticks and my bare hands to dig it up. My brothers waited in annoyance. At last, I pulled out the beauty. Clouds seem trapped inside what appeared to be an oversized diamond. I thought it was worth a fortune until my dad broke the bad news. "That's basically a piece of glass." I've moved that silly piece of glass with me more than a dozen times since.
I see it as a symbol of my own inner determination.

Although, I've never survived an almost fatal crash or fought for freedom. I've seen what true determination looks like. It's fierce. When Hector Roman went to state the school year he started diving again I couldn't believe it. I told my news director we had to go. *We had to be there.* I fulfilled my promise to Hector. The photographer and I traveled to Austin and documented this full circle moment. Hector didn't win first place. *He didn't even make top three.* He placed somewhere in the top ten. This wasn't a fairytale or news ending. This was the real life end to an almost tragic story. Hector pushed through the pain, showed passion, purpose and unfathomable determination while staying humble. I am grateful he and his family for allowing me to bear witness to this extraordinary feat of will.

> Affirmation:
> Determination takes patience. I find comfort and strength in every step, as I work toward my goals.

Chapter 45: I'll always have NATS

"Realize deeply that the present moment is all you have. Make the NOW the primary focus of your life." – Eckhart Tolle

A sibilant symphony poured out of the coffee maker. Brandon tapped a wooden spoon and the morning news set the beat. I listened and smiled. I may not work in news anymore but I will always have NATS otherwise known as natural sound. I tried to pepper all of my stories with amazing natural sound. Just like pops of soulful color these sounds make a 90 second story more interesting.

Eckhart Tolle wrote about the importance of paying attention to the moment in his book *The Power of Now.* I read it during college and remember focusing extra attention at my part-time serving job. I listened as ice clanged in the cup, soda fizzed and plates hit the counter. Everyday sounds and sensations hold the power to anchor me to the here and now. After years of practice listening to sounds out in the field and the edit bay as a reporter, I now hear NATS in the shower, on a walk or while cleaning. I visualize a tight camera shot of my hands as I switch off a rush of water while doing the dishes.

In those micro-moments I feel the pulse of life. Brandon's breath on his pillow or a sweet little trumpet like toot can signal a sigh or giggle. I listen for the NATS and my eyes open wide.

I probably can't list everything I learned as a reporter but I will try. I've learned that every story showcases infinite sides not just two.

I've learned to lead with respect and compassion (people who forget post selfies in front of caskets or fires).

I've learned that following up is more important than the initial call. I've learned that weakness is sometimes strength. The best sound bites aren't rehearsed. Hearts understand real and raw over contrived and fake. Peace takes more courage than warfare.

Reputation matters. I've learned that sometimes calling every name in a phone book or knocking on every door is what it takes. I've learned that not everyone will dial every number or knock on every door. I've learned it never hurts to ask. I've learned that all people want to feel both unique and ordinary. I've learned that the image of Jesus appearing on anything is a probably a story. I've learned that no matter what some women won't go on camera if their hair isn't done. I've learned men cry too. I've learned that hard times happen. I've learned that the news business is small. Gossip needs to end with me. I've learned you can't please everyone. I've learned somewhere out there a little old lady hates my necklace and my hair and the cut of my dress and the way I pronounce the word cement. And that's ok!

I've learned there will be those days when I lose my shoe in the mud or get pen on my eyelid moments before going live or fall out of a news unit but everything, will be Bob Marley "alright." I can't go back to the stress of news deadlines right now, I'm afraid my aura depends on it. I will always have NATS— and the love of a good story.

> Affirmation:
> I listen for the sounds and sensations of the everyday in order to live a more soulful life.

Chapter 46: Letter to Brandon

"Through the blur, I wondered if I was alone or if other parents felt the same way I did - that everything involving our children was painful in some way. The emotions, whether they were joy, sorrow, love or pride, were so deep and sharp that in the end they left you raw, exposed and yes, in pain. The human heart was not designed to beat outside the human body and yet, each child represented just that - a parent's heart bared, beating forever outside its chest." -Debra Ginsberg

Dear Brandon,

I love you so, you lovely little soul. I hope you're reading this and your future self is rolling your eyes thinking "I know, mom." Good. I am glad you know. I hope you have a little brother or sister and I hope they know too. My goal is to model the lessons I've written about in such a way that you can't ignore them even if you're getting ready to leave the house. Please, remember to let go of worry. Believe you're worthy. Laugh at yourself. Enjoy the thrill of not knowing what's coming next in life. Choose goodness. Try. Let fear lead you. Listen. Let joy lead you. Listen. Your interpretation of these messages will shape your life in beautiful or destructive ways. You must choose.

I pray I am still around to be with you. I wish you a long life but please know your time is limited. Set your sights higher than getting by. Enjoy every day. This life was meant for you. You edged out 200 million other little souls to get here. Please know I feel like I won the lottery with you.

Please, please take care of yourself. Take care of my little boy.

Wear your seatbelt. Get flood insurance.

Drink water. Replace the batteries on your smoke detector. Pray. Eat vegetables. Drive Sober. Be friendly. Be kind. Be cautious. Get everything in writing. Save more money than you spend. Travel anywhere, as often as you can afford. Celebrate small victories. Play for fun. Challenge yourself. Only obsess about inner beauty. Be sure to get that inner beauty sleep too. Move your body to quiet your mind. Keep your receipts. Learn new skills on the job whenever possible. Learn new skills in life whenever possible. Fret about the people you love. Fuss over the extras in life. Someday the people you love won't be there for you to fuss over. If you're going to order ranch, order it on the side. Skip soda. Drink water. Make your bed. Iron your clothes before you put them away. Wash your fruit right away. Do laundry often. Splurge once-in-a while. Use those things you splurge on every day. Everyday matters. Everyday should be an event. Remember you are made of stardust. That makes you immeasurably powerful and paradoxically nothing more than dust. Remember, deep breaths are free all day long.

    I understand this letter is futile. You must live and figure this all out for yourself in your own time. You will find many spiritual teachers along the way. Hold onto the messages that resonate with you and make sense to you. There are thousands of raindrops but only one way down from the heavens. It's simple. Seek. Open. Let go. Stay present. Love. That's it. Choose the journey and share your experience and your gifts. You are loved, as you are! You are and will always be the best thing that's ever happened to me.
Love,
Your mom

> Reporter's Notepad:
> What is something you wish your parents would have said to you growing up?
> Are there any words you need to hear in order to heal any lingering childhood wounds?

Chapter 47: Ever Happily After

"They say a person needs just three things to be truly happy in this world: someone to love, something to do, and something to hope for." –Tom Bodett

I've taken a very long writing hiatus. I haven't written anything in months. Really, I've done this to avoid editing. I've also felt like my writing is terrible and no one will read it anyway. Could I be any more typical? I am *supposed* to be editing. I am not really an editor. I WANT TO CAPITALIZE everything and throw periods in willy-nilly. Who wants to edit? I want to gripe, emote and leave my baggage unpacked on the page. Of course, "ain't nobody got time for that." I must respect the time of anyone willing to read my...well, my crap. I would be editing now, perhaps. Except, there's just one thing— *a lot* has happened since I last documented my life. I wrote a sweet letter to my baby boy. Now I am expecting his little sister! Brandon also broke his leg. He was on my hip and his shoe became caught on the passenger car seat as I reached for his water bottle. He wore a cast for two weeks. As you would imagine, I'm still cast in guilt.

Thankfully for me, he knocked his teeth on the nightstand on my husband's watch a month or so later. It was the worst day of my life. Brandon screamed with his mouth full of blood as the dentist yanked out a dangling baby tooth. I tried to keep my composure—I didn't want this to be about my fears for him.

Those fears trickled out anyway. I cried for my baby as I wrapped my arms around him and tried to keep him from moving. We were shaking.

It was AWFUL. Then a few days after the trauma I wondered why didn't I take those family photos sooner? We were exhausted from the ordeal and we felt like lousy parents. How did this happen? Like all things—they just do. This year I've dealt with ear infections, colds, and an epic 18-hour-overnight trek from Fresno to Phoenix to Dallas to San Antonio with a sick toddler. Needless to say, one delay turned into many. Brandon's started saying words. He can say apple, truck, car and farts! Boys. I am overjoyed by the news of our little girl.

The new baby's due date will mean I will miss my beloved cousin's wedding in August. That's a disappointing reality. I've missed so many events for so many people I love and feel connected to over the years; first, because I wanted to pursue my dreams as a reporter and now because I am living life with a family (on a budget). This year I will miss three major weddings and my brother's graduation. I can blame money, time and pregnancy.

2015 is about managing many a meltdown (most of them Brandon's) and swapping early morning grunts with my husband as we decide who will get up and play with Brandon at 5:45AM. I've also been working part-time learning how to write grants and fundraise for a local affiliate of an international non-profit. It's great experience and I'm glad I've had the chance. I still feel like I fall short. I don't work full-time so I don't make enough, I also don't spend enough time at home and I haven't figured out how to truly fit myself into the equation. I'm in the thick of motherhood and marriage and I can see only the faintest vision of a clearing in about 5 or 20 years.

I've let the rigmarole of life steamroll over my joy over the last few months.

I've also pushing my writing goals aside as I deal with the everyday. Maybe that's how I ended up in a Dunkin Donut pestering a teenage cashier about why "I didn't get the donut I ordered!" I'd gone through the drive-thru moments earlier. "What do you mean you don't have a plain chocolate bar? I don't want an Éclair!" I felt like a toddler stopping in her rain boots. I can hear the 2 year old inside of me too. "Éclair, no fair!" Pouty-face. Clouds congregate in the skies outside. I felt like one of those crazy women on TV desperately calling 911 because McDonald's ran out of chicken nuggets. Clearly, this was a low point. Clearly, I'd learned nothing in my quest to cleanse my aura and reflect on being an amazingly present and calm mother.

Of course, this was not about the donuts. I wanted the experience. Even if they'd gotten it right the order wouldn't have filled me up. I craved the taste I remembered on Sunday mornings at my Abuela's house. A long chocolate bar with frosting and no filling! I wanted time travel or a trip home—a memory long gone. I've watched so many of my old friendships and relationships shift and change due to the changes I've made in my life. Many parenting books warn about changing relationships coinciding with changing life stages. I didn't think my friendships would change. Thankfully, a few friends are mired in this exact stage of life as me. We're able to connect and for that I am grateful.

Memories fascinate me. Why do I remember donuts on Sundays? Siegel and Bryson talk about memory retrieval. They say once we've retrieved a memory we've moved it into a different location in the brain.

This happens each and every time we rent the same memory. Just like an old Blockbuster Video Rental with bad service— it gets restocked on a different shelf every time. Therefore, we can't really trust our memories unconditionally. *Sometimes we remember things as better than they really were.*

Brian Williams learned that the hard way. However, I will say I love him unconditionally. He helped me get over my fear of live shots along with the help of a tall West Texas Sheriff who used forensic hypnosis to ease my anxiety. Williams helped by stumbling over his words on live TV moments before I was set to go live on the local NBC affiliate. Standing on a lot with a wind-ravaged trailer home behind me, the former anchor's mistake helped me relax. Everyone makes mistakes. *Everyone.* This wasn't about me or my nerves anyway. I was there to share what happened and hope someone might help.

Miss-remembering isn't reserved for Williams. I miss-remembered a childhood trauma and lived to tell the story over and over until my mother corrected me. Here's my version: my thumb was black and blue after I slammed it....in something (I won't even try.) I remember the sound of the drill as my mom revved it up, prepped my nail with alcohol and started drilling. I can hear the sound!

Nope, according to my mom I made this up. She claims it was a *drill bit* and she never turned on anything. She slowly twisted the metal bit into my nail just to relieve the pressure.

Don't I feel silly? I hope Brandon's recent traumas at the dentist and with his leg don't get amplified in some dark storage vault in his mind. I am going to try to use the strategies of the *Whole Brain Child* and *No Drama Discipline* to help him integrate the "big feelings" he must have felt.

I wish he didn't have to feel them though. (Leave it to a mom to want to protect a child from his own feelings). I guess I need to learn how to soothe my own anxiety when Brandon learns to deal with pain of any kind. I must accept that feelings and emotions are necessary for a connected life and in healthy relationships.

    I've felt so many feelings now that I am pregnant again. Two kids. Two years apart. The big feelings I've been feeling have prompted some pretty crazy dreams. I dreamed I interviewed Oprah Winfrey. The dream was either something I've heard her say in an interview or perhaps my subconscious hard at work. I sat on a director style chair in a very softly lit studio. "Did you envision all of this for yourself in the truest sense?" I asked. "No, I knew things would be big but I would never as a little girl have believed all of this." She said adding, "I needed to dream a dream large enough to fill the space I was in. As the space changed and grew... my dreams needed to expand. The dreams needed to be big but attainable. Therefore, as our dreams are fulfilled we must make sure the dreams keep growing right along with us." I thought about this idea for days. Did my own dreams fill the space around me?

    I gave a presentation to a local Cinematography class after my Oprah dream awakened something inside me. I told the kids to submit for every contest, every film festival, and take every chance along the way. I said "in order to hear 'yes' they'd need to hear a lot of 'no's.'" I spoke eloquently and passionately and gave good advice.

    I needed to hear the words I summoned from someplace forgotten. Maybe, I freaked out about the éclair because I wanted to go back and remember what it felt like to be young and inspired.

I haven't wanted to edit and I haven't wanted to write. In fact, I sorted my documents by file date and one document was written "earlier this year" and all the others were "written a long time ago." It's time to reengage. I let setbacks; and fears of rejection dominate the space meant for my dreams.

My husband and I finally took those family pictures, today. The pictures didn't go exactly as planned but we enjoyed taking them. Brandon showed off a huge mosquito bite right between his eyes. My husband and I were sweating. B is still missing a tooth. I felt super pregnant. After the photo-sesh we ended up losing our way before pulling out the GPS to find a bakery we'd always wanted to try. Outside Bakery Loraine we strolled through the farmer's market we didn't expect to find. Later in the day my boys got a nap, I got a little time to relax and WRITE and we swam at the neighborhood pool after that. I felt at peace with my life again. The great lessons I most want to teach Brandon are those I still need to practice. I am sure I will see clouds move in around me again. I am certain the sun will come out not too long after.

I no longer believe the myth of family and marriage perpetuated by fairy tales. Marriage and family can't erase uncertainty from my life.

Some of my single friends have actually said "I wish my life was as easy as yours." If only! I find more uncertainty in family life now.

The variables have increased exponentially and I have so much more to lose. This gives me more reason to fall in love with the moment, nurture my creativity and elevate my energy.

I will go on trying to teach Brandon the great lessons of love, persistence, determination, and happiness.

My guess; he'll teach me far more. He's already reminding me to say my prayers, to laugh often and to love with all that I am.

> Takeaway:
>
> Happiness is not a finish line you cross and forever claim your place in the winner's circle...it's a practice. Lessons must be lived. Keep calm and love on my friends!

References:

Althea Solter, P. (2015, September 21). *The Aware Parenting Institute*. Retrieved from www.awareparenting.com: http://www.awareparenting.com/solter.htm

Becker, G. D. (1998). *The Gift of Fear and Other Survival Signals that Protect Us From Violence.* New York: Random House.

Brown, D. B. (2012). *Daring Greatly: How the Courage to Be Vulnerable Transforms the Way We Live, Love, Parent, and Lead.* New York: Gotham Books.

Bryne, R. (2006). *The Secret.* New York: Atria Books.

Bryson, D. D. (2011). *The Whole-Brain Child: 12 Revolutionary Strategies to Nurture Your Child's Developing Mind.* New York: Delecorte Press.

Bryson, D. D. (2015). *No-Drama Discipline: The Whole-Brain Way to Calm the Chaos and Nurture Your Child's Developing.* New York: Bantam.

Buffet, W. (2013, November 17). CBS 60 Minutes. (C. Rose, Interviewer)

Cherie Carter-Scott, P. (1998). *If Life is a Game, These are the Rules.* New York: MJF Books.

Gladwell, M. (2015). *Blink: The Power of Thinking Without Thinking.* New York: Back Bay Books.

Hal Runkel, I. (2007). *Screamfree Parenting.* New York: Broadway Books.

Hanh, T. N. (2012). OWN Network. (O. Winfrey, Interviewer)

Kinder, G. (1999). *7 Stages of Money Maturity.* New York: Dell Publishing.

McGraw, D. P. (2013, May 19). Oprah and Dr. Phil: How to Play Big and Be the Star of Your Own Life. (O. Winfrey, Interviewer)

Parrott, L. a. (1995). *Saving Your Marriage Before It Starts: Seven Questions to Ask Before You Marry .* Grand Rapids : Zondervan.

Piven, J. (1999). *Worst Case Scenario.* San Francisco: Chronicle Books.

Risley, B. H. (2003). "The Early Catastrophe: The 30 Million Word Gap by Age 3". *American Educator*, 6-9.

Roberts, R. (2014, June 15). Oprah's Master Class. (R. Roberts, Interviewer)

Ruiz, M. (1997). *The Four Agreements.* San Rafael: Amber-Allen Publishing.

Soukup, R. (2014). *Living Well, Spending Less: 12 Secerts of the Good Life.* Grand Rapids: Zondervan.

Tolle, E. (1999). *The Power of Now.* Novato: New World Library.

Turlington, C. (2002). *Living Yoga: Creating a Life of Practice.* New York: Hyperion.

Wade, B. (2014, February 12). The View. (J. M. Elliot, Interviewer)

Williamson, M. (1996). *A Return to Love: Reflections on the Principles of "A Course In Miracles".* New York: Harper One.

Zukav, G. (1989). *Seat of the Soul.* New York: Simon and Schuster.

About the Author: Camaron D. Brooks spent more than five years covering stories in the Rio Grande Valley and the Midland/Odessa television markets before starting her family. She covered everything from crime, teenage pregnancy, homelessness, border and family violence. She hopes her experiences as a general assignment reporter/anchor and new mother inspire other women to live mindfully and joyfully. She believes self-improvement and learning are life-long endeavors. Camaron lives with her growing family in San Antonio, Texas.

Thank you dear reader! I can't tell you what it means to me that you picked up my life story and read through the entire thing. I hope you didn't cringe too much while reading all of my embarrassing moments and hopefully you got something out of it the lessons I've learned. Remember it all takes practice. If you enjoyed this book please consider writing a review and tell a friend. (Reviews help indie authors share their work with more readers.) I'm so grateful for your support. Again, I hope you found this book to be enjoyable, helpful and soul-stirring. Sending lots of love and light.

Sincerely, *Camaron Brooks*

Acknowledgements: First and foremost, I must thank God. I am grateful for all the open *and closed* doors I've knocked on in my life. Thank you for continuing to guide my life into motherhood. Thank you to my loving parents, Oscar and Janet you've made all of this possible for me. Thank you to my grandparents John and Ellen Edwards and Aurora and Antonio Abundes†. Thank you to my-in-laws Elizabeth and Donald T. Brooks†.

I would like to thank my brothers Aaron and Adrian along with my sister-in-laws Lizette and Jessica. Cover photo credit Jessica Abundes. Thank you, Jess! You are so talented. My nephews and niece Mateo, Lucca and Olivia. I must thank a slew of friends, some I get the chance to see and some I only get the chance to think and pray about. Thank you to Jenny Huey for being there through thick and thin. Thank you to Stephanie Bertini for encouraging me to finish this project and for always making me laugh and living your dreams so others might do the same.

Thank you to all of the amazing beautiful women who've graced my life in and out of the newsroom, including but not limited to; Frances Becerra, Lindsay Marks, Alice Livingston, Andrea Mrazova-Rybova, Robyn Licari, Anna Lagomarsino-Bowman, Jillian Devine, Loreen Huey, Melissa Osuna, Sarah Sutman, Cassie Price, Jennifer Alverson, Saody Freeman, Cassandra Maynard, Alicia Dobales, Susette Simas, Desirae Allen, Erica Proffer and Catia Holm, Carrie Libert, Mandy Westly and all the moms of the NW San Antonio Playgroup.

Big thank you to Stephanie Gracia, Sarah White, Jaqueline Keakulina, Shawndrea Thomas, Emily Baucum, Crystal Cruz, Pamela Hamm, Lisa Cortez, Emily Cecil, Katie Lopez-Haris, Nina Pruneda, Annie, Pruneda, Samantha Newbold, Sandra Salinas, Maggie Kosub, Hema Muller, Farah Fazal, Maureen Mahoney, Jackie Trevino, Heather Flores, Dina-Herrera Garza, Letty Garza, Stephanie Becerra, Stephanie Zepelin, Shelley Childers, Francesca Canote, Melinda Foster, Mandi Bice, Sabrina Morris, Renee Estargiau, Jessica Farnoccia Shulz, Janine Santos Dooley, Roma Vivas, Magaly Nieto, Rachel Macintyre, Evette De Hoyas, Lindsey Johnson and all of my friends with the NW Mommy Playgroup, Maggie Reed, Kristen Pettineo, Mitzi Loera, Cristina Lozano, Tyresa Saski, Tina Battiati, Coral Reyes, Cori Pope, Genevieve Reyes, Audrey Palacios, Renee Sour, Renee La Salle, Katherine Daniels and Melissa Correa. I would also like to thank Heather Ash, Sonia Beatrice and friends new and old.

I must thank all of my aunts and uncles; Tony Abundes, Violet Borrego-Abundes, and Claude Jones and Aurora Abundes-Jones. Sharon and Chris Victor, Katherine and Dave Dandridge, Diane and Dan Bewley, Michael and Val Edwards, Bryce and Beth Edwards. I love you all dearly. You're the best and have made my life so rich! Thank you to all of my cousins for being my best friends and for growing into such amazing people; Darrah Borrego, Vincent Borrego, Samuel Borrego, Erin Elizabeth Victor, Maggie Victor, Allison Flanders, Emma Dandridge, Page Edwards, Will Edwards, Grant Edwards, Rachel Edwards, Savannah Edwards, Benjamin Bewley, Joshua Jones and Maya Jones. Plus, I must thank a wide net of extended family all over the country and world.

I would like to thank my husband's sisters Vickie Herrington and Teresa Jones and his Brother Donnie. I would like to thank all of the people who made me a better reporter and person. News Directors Mark Kurtz, Jenny Martinez, Marta Waller and Tony Valdez thank you for encouraging me and pushing me to find my strengths.

Assistant News Director David Silva, thank you for bringing levity into an often chaotic environment. Assignment Editor Raul Castelan for being yourself Caste!

Thank you to Rick Stewart, Arturo Vargas, Izzy Alfaro Enrique Saenz, Justin Michelle, Trenton Downey, Mike Hughes, JV Villarreal, Dennis Thomas, Ken Koller, Christian Garcia, Jody Powers, Gene De La Cruz, Rudy Jaquez, Bill Taylor, Victor Lopez, Stephanie Miranda, Marcos Montes, Jerry Lee Berg and Tammy Meyers along with John Kittleman.

Also thanks to Jordan Williams, Rick Diaz, Oscar Adame, Polo Sandoval, Bill Barajas, Joe Augustine, Antonio Lujan, Will Ripley and Wyatt Goolsby for your excellent work and example as human beings. I know there are more to acknowledge here!

Thank you to Danny Tarantine and the gang at Papalucci's. Thank you to Natalie Griffith and Stephanie Wiese for teaching me the importance of devoting your life to the service of others. I've learned so much during the last year. Thank you to Ashley Marsh, Noelle Pinto and Trisch Nolan for giving me a chance to work on a creative team again.

Thank you to the Busalacchis, DeAndas, Livseys and McMurrans. It was a pleasure growing up with our families so intertwined. You're always in my heart.

I would like to thank all of the great teachers I've been blessed to learn from over the years including Beth Bingham, Bob Hersh, Ray Burton, Donald Knudsen and Ruben Modesto, and many many others.

I would like to thank Tatiana Villa from Villa Design for creating the cover of this book and for Maureen Cutajar from Go Published for assisting me in this process with my ebook. Also big thank you to Alyssa Martin!! I really appreciate your support. I couldn't have done this without your help. Thanks to Angie Teage from Angie Teage Photography and Ashlee Rice from Let's Face It Makeup Studio you all are amazing!

Thank you to Brandon and Addison for allowing me to document these shenanigans. I LOVE YOU!! And most of all thank you to Donald S. Brooks. You've encouraged me and put up with my writing obsession. Just two more minutes!! *Famous last line*. I am so grateful for your love and support! I would not be the woman I am today without you. I love you in every way. Thank you!!!!!

Kicker: An Afterward About Thrills, Frills, and Wishes

"The best way to teach a child is live an exemplary life." –Lailah Gifty Akita

Pink pom-poms now hang in the nursery, and Brandon's old closet is packed with tutus and frilly dresses. The Brooks household is once again aflutter as we welcome the arrival of our baby girl. Meeting my daughter was one of the thrills of my life. I feel silly writing an afterward, holding my new baby and once again planning to stay home full-time for the next year. I know so much lies ahead. The same lessons, affirmations, and takeaways I've shared will no doubt come in handy for me over the course of Addison's first year. I know I need to breathe and stay present.

My wish for my little girl, above all else, is that she be brave. I hope I'm brave enough to be her mother. I want her to find adventure and love in her life, and that she's dazzled by simple pleasures and undaunted by the expectations of this world. I remember the little girl in me who wanted to touch a waterfall at Yosemite National Park. My father nearly called the park ranger when my aunt and I shimmied around a steep cliff in search of a beautiful cascade. Forget the song; I absolutely want her to chase waterfalls, fireflies, and her dreams.

Our story will go on beyond the reflections and lessons I've recorded. I am certain I will make more realizations and mistakes.

I will keep examining myself and studying this whole parenting thing. (I just started reading *The Danish Way of Parenting*.)

I'll do my absolute best to stay attuned to this moment and the love in my heart. I will forgive myself when I don't rise to meet the magnitude of the role. I will celebrate all the new little things I'll experience with a daughter: giggles, frilly bows, and pink dresses. All those things, my brown eyed girl will one day leave behind.

Maybe beginnings are really endings masquerading as new. I can only thank God and hold onto the moment I'm experiencing right now—like the thrill of watching my little girl's personality blossom right alongside her brothers. I will go back to work and the kids will grow up all too soon. It's a privilege to report to the Brook's family dining table each morning, noon and night (even if it means sweeping up crumbs and wiping sticky hands afterwards).

Kicker #3: Life's Full of Surprises

I am sitting here typing (pregnant again!)My third child is due in 2017. This book (like a gorgeous aunt pointed out) is a little like a baby too. I've loved sharing my stories and seeing it in paperback will be a dream-come-true! Seriously, could rank among my top favorite things that's ever happened in my life. I want to continue writing books for moms and kids. I want to share my journey because—
while the struggle is real— *so is the joy!*

My goal here is share Studio Baby with more readers. That's why I've made it available in print with a few minor tweaks and bonuses!

That's all my mindset needed too. *Minor tweaks.* I am focused on the good. I am more focused on the joyful and less on how difficult life with small children can be. (Stay tuned.)

Bonus Material from Reportinglivefromstudiob.com

Why I am Not Ready for Mom's Night Out

I stepped into the Magic Time Machine without a diaper bag. A woman dressed as Disney's Jasmine handed me a menu. Teal harem paints framed a toned porcelain tummy. She must not have kids, I thought. Marks formed over two pregnancies now wind around my belly like a mountainside eroded by rain. My midriff wasn't the only thing forced to stretch. I'm a nursing, baby-food making, toilet-training, mom of two. Yep, it's a whole new world. *And I'm tired.* That's why agreed to a mom's night out. *Freedom might feel like a magic carpet ride.*

I looked over the entrees, skipping the kid section. *How will I eat without a baby in my lap?* I've held my daughter for six-months now. She's an 18 pound delight. Sometimes after I strap her into the baby Bjorn, my 33 pound toddler wants me to hold him too. "Mommy attention!" *How can I say no?* He jumps on, straddling my hip, as I haul 50 or so extra pounds. Motherhood. Sitting alone in the waiting area I started wondering how they were doing. Did Brandon brush his teeth? Did Addy fall asleep?

Soon Buddy the Elf took us on a tour of the restaurant. At the table, I confessed to the other moms I might cry. I missed my baby (both of my babies really).

"The baby stage is so short" I lamented. I remember feeling like the baby stage would never end with my son.

The fatigue felt unending. Then one day he started picking out his own clothes and telling me he didn't like my choice of music in the car.

Brandon blows kisses my way and says "okay, bye" when I leave.

I won't let the fatigue fool me the second time around. The baby stage will end and very soon. Addison no longer wants to be wrapped tightly against my body at all times. She's enjoying her adventures on the ground. She rolls and moves. She's ready to take off. I feel it. My daughter is changing so fast I can almost measure her growth in moments. (Moments I quit my job, rearranged my body and whole life to experience.)

The other moms and I chatted about our families over appetizers, laughed at the ridiculous personas of the wait staff and enjoyed the tranquility of dining without children. I relaxed. I almost felt like a woman and not a mom. The food arrived and then the checks. Buddy the Elf serenaded us. Then I noticed six missed calls from my husband. "Six missed calls! I gotta go." I said bye as I pressed the call button on my cell. I could hear the cries. My baby missed me.

I made it home in fourteen minutes. My husband said Addy tired herself out and fell asleep before I burst through the door. Red blotches left a rim around her face. I whispered "I'm so sorry." My husband assured me she was fine. He changed her, fed her and bounced her. She just wanted her mom. *I am so privileged to be her mom.*

I can visit the Magic Time Machine anytime I want a shrimp scampi. I can't kick time off its tracks. Sometimes I want to take a bullet train to an age where these tiny people can make their own eggs. I can't do that either. I agreed to a mom's night out before I was truly ready. Before my baby was ready.

I will happily jump off of the train for another mom's night out down the line probably at the next milestone when Addy's favorite word is "no" and I fully understand the whole backpack leash thing. Until then, I'm snuggling. I'm savoring. I'm staying in.

Pride, Ego and the Plastic Pineapple

I sat on a park bench, one sweet Saturday afternoon, swapping humble boasts— bonding over motherhood. The woman next to me cooed at my baby and praised my toddler's fearlessness on the slide. My pride beamed like October sunshine until my son shoved a little girl to the ground. The little girl's mom shouted "No! That's unacceptable." Shame sent my heart tumbling. I felt attacked. In a haze of embarrassment and remorse I walked over and started quizzing my son. What happened? What did she do? She must have done something. That mom didn't need to use such a violent tone.

Brandon fessed up to pushing the little girl and my husband assured me it was indeed unprovoked. My vision blurred. Anger enveloped. "It's okay" the mom muttered in response to my flimsy apology from across the park. I waived bye to my new friend and pushed my daughter's stroller away briskly as my husband and son hurried to catch up. Blame spewed like a broken sewer line in my head. Why did my son do that? That mom had no right to speak to Brandon that way. Where did he learn to shove? He did NOT learn it from me. I am a good mom. I shoved down bitter insecurity, wishing for absolution.
slide

I'd forgotten about the shoving episode until I started reading *The Conscious Parent.* Dr. Shefali Tsabary explains how parents can easily wander off into the realm of ego. (The ego of image, perfection or control. I stood squarely in the ego of image at the park.) I let my toddler's bad choice and normal behaviour make me feel like a bad mom.

I made it about me. I felt judged. Flustered by my own emotions and feelings of inadequacy I severed an opportunity to teach.

Dr. Tsabary writes "life is wise." In its absolute wisdom life served up another chance for me to enter into ego a few months later at the zoo. Bonding with a friend over motherhood, I heard sobs from another little girl. I didn't take the bait. Brandon had snatched a plastic pineapple (the very symbol of hospitality and friendship) out of her hands. This little girl sobbed as her mother whisked her away too quickly. I went over to my son and asked him what happened. I didn't feel threatened. I felt compassionate. Brandon's eyes widened with empathy. This was not about me. I welcomed the opportunity to teach. "We don't snatch. We share. You made that little girl cry. Let's go say sorry?" He nodded.

We raced through double doors down a windy path toward a trail of loud tears. I knelt down and prompted Brandon softly. He offered a sturdy apology. The little's girl mom looked surprised. "Tell him you forgive him," she encouraged.

"I forgive you," the little girl said still crying. Her words hovered in my head for days. I forgive you. The words delivered a wallop of perspective.
In response to an apology, I might have prompted my son to say "it's okay or don't worry about it" but the little girl at the zoo knew better. It's not okay to hurt others with our actions. If we do, we must learn to apologize from a pure place and we can only hope our heartfelt apology is met with raw forgiveness. I witnessed this powerful message only after I checked my emotions at the exit doors. Life is truly, unrelentingly wise.

I can't undo my behaviour at the park nor can I offer a heartfelt apology to the little girl and mom I mentally slandered.

(It's clearly impossible to learn a lesson while defensively yielding a three pronged pitch fork of pride, ego and perfectionism.)

I can only show up consciously moving forward and pray I can catch all the lessons life shoves my way.

Great Confrontations

I thought the days of getting kicked out of just about anywhere ended when I left TV news. Tracking down some funeral home owner accused of mismanaging funds, or some district attorney charged with taking bribes is no longer part of the routine (not that I ever liked confrontation). My new routine involves play dates, trips to the park and potty training (ironically, *now I'm the one dishing out bribes*).

Brandon earns "special gum" for a successful trip to the toilet. Of course successful is a relative term. He can pee on the bathroom floor and still get special gum. He's pretty proud of his new undies and when he needs to go, it's truly an urgent matter (like drop your pants in the middle of a mall food court urgent). We were noshing on pretzels when he nearly whipped out his a few weeks ago. *No one told me how fun this would be or how long it would take.* I can barely keep track of when I need to pee and now I'm in charge of keeping track of his urges (and cleaning up after them too.)

This is by far my least favorite motherhood chore. Especially, after last week. I kicked through puddles of shame as I faced one of the most mortifying confrontations of my life. It happened at a park in a friend's neighborhood. Brandon played, the baby slept and all was well until I heard the phrase "mommy, I need to go pee-pee."

I scooped him up and headed toward the bathroom. *Okay, we've got this.* Then I noticed a keypad lock on the door.

My friend didn't know the code. The park was teaming with kids and parents.

I went back around to the front of the building.

I knew how urgently he needed to pee. He probably needed to go twenty minutes before ever verbalizing it. *This was serious.* Why didn't I ask him? Why didn't I scope out the scene before he needed to pee? Why didn't I have an extra pair of pants? *Oh, look some bushes.*

  I gave him the O.K. The area appeared empty. I didn't know what else to do. I looked around like a crook trying to dodge reporters. That's when I noticed an office window and employees gazing in disbelief (mouths gapping and all). My son's Thomas The Train underpants sounded the alarm.

  "Ma'am, this is private property. This is unacceptable," an employee said after exiting her office space. "Do you live here? What homeowner are you with? Why didn't you ask us for the code?"

  "I'm so sorry," I said, eager to give my side of the story. "He's two and potty training. I didn't know what else to do. I had no idea this was an office. You have kids right? I am so sorry. We'll be leaving."

  The woman softened and admitted she raised boys. I still wanted to hide in the
bushes. Motherhood aims to humble. I'd like to say no one warned me but they did. I just didn't listen. I thought TV news was glamorous and exciting before I started. Professors warned me then too. I didn't listen (and I'm glad). I found my strength in a small market newsroom. I cried every night for at least a month. The tears returned with the weight of responsibility when we brought our son home from the hospital.
I won't ever like confrontations or potty training but I can appreciate the hard days a little more lately (the fussy days, the tired days, the days I wish I could tell my younger self to rest up for or even the *not funny enough to blog about days*).

Those days matter too. I can sit with another mom and tell her "I understand." I can warn expectant moms that it's not all snuggles and sing-a-longs. Although, I know they shouldn't listen. Let them confront a new level of humility, strength and invincible love waiting at the end of their worst days. I know I have. And who knows? I'll probably do it again tomorrow (we are still potty training.)

The Phrase I Banished from Our Home

My toddler slides a guitar strap around his neck. His fubsy fingers strum a choppy tune as I smile from the couch. Maybe he'll become a musician and escort his dear old mom to the Grammys. "Bradley Cooper took his to the Oscars," I'll joke. A funny face can trigger an equally audacious thought about a comedy career. His love for heavy-duty construction equipment somehow means he'll one day build houses for a living. Kids play pretend. Parents, we do too.

We all want to see our kids cultivate amazing lives for themselves. We've got eighteen years and the end game is a happy, healthy, kind and productive adult.

The more I mutter the phrase, "He's going to be," the more I realize it's tied to a unquenchable desire for security. I want to know I'm guiding him toward his best life. That I'm doing a good job. I don't know what he will be. I only know what he is. He's a wonderful, sweet, funny, intense, energetic boy. However, I dishonor the moment and teach him to over-value the future by prognosticating. The phrase also burdens him with unnecessary expectations. He can be anything he dreams (although, I realize that's not always true).

It wasn't true for a lovely teammate on my high school basketball team who died of an asthma attack. It wasn't true for a good friend, who left us after crash on a rainy road near her house in 2002. Lives don't last forever. This truth clobbered my psyche as I worked as a general assignment reporter. Heartbroken mothers and fathers used different phrases "She's never going to be... He's never going to do..."

Obviously, it's easier to turn my thoughts toward bright fantasies and exciting futures for my kids. It's easier to pretend they're mine to keep...that they're promised eighteen years and then some. My daughter and son are only promised now (just like the rest of us). The awareness stings. I make promises to the present moment; to flip around to see a front-end loader on the side of the road, to laugh at silly jokes after a long day. It persuades me to pay attention to the same incoherent tune, over and over and not to say "He's going to be" or "She's going to do..." The truth asks me not to worry but rather to adoringly hold their little hands knowing it's all in God's (The Grammy's and grandkids included).

Mindful Breathing Hack for (Sometimes Angry) Moms

Life with a toddler is like riding on a revolving see-saw all day long. UP. DOWN. ALL. AROUND. My head spins trying to keep it together. The other day my son wildly pecked and pawed at my laptop keyboard. "He's literally pushing my buttons," I told my husband later. The power struggle is real my friends. I'm doing my best to control my own emotions. I'm casting my attention to parenting books aimed at helping me **stay present** in the joyful waves while trying to **stay calm** during the daily lows. Brandon's second birthday ushered in a surge of personality, demands and feelings. The swell of his new sense of self— challenges me every day. He's so unpredictable. Sometimes he's sweet and communicative. Sometimes, inexplicably, he stops using real words. He ditches the spoon in favor of shoving rice into his mouth by the fistful. Then there's the screaming. That little barbarian leads me straight to the swamps of my reactive, primitive brain (the crazy leaks out).

I recently picked up *10 Mindful Minutes* Author/Actor Goldie Hawn does a great job of illustrating *real* techniques used to teach children and parents about mindfulness. The work of the Hawn Foundation through its Mind UP Program is remarkable. In her book she explains practices like mindful breathing, mindful sensing, and mindful movement in everyday language. The guide provides research backed information quoting experts like Dr. Dan Siegel.

His books helped me sort out feelings when I first documented my struggle, transitioning from my career into motherhood. In times of stress, I've turned to mindful breathing over the years. However, I've always felt as graceful as a bull *especially now*. By the tenth time "Be gentle," turns into me breathlessly shouting "STOP hitting your sister!" Angry sighs are all I can muster. My sanity ebbs. In these moments, breathing is the only buoy. Yet, I'm reactive not meditative.

I can tell you, I NEVER expected to feel anger on a consistent basis as a mother. I guess that's why this quote and question from *"10 Mindful Minutes"* was so eye opening: "It is well noted that anger is only fear in disguise….Have you ever experienced anger when your child runs into the street to retrieve a ball without thinking?"

Absolutely. No matter the scenario if Brandon is in danger I'm awash with fear *and anger.*

I've watched Brandon jump from the ottoman to the couch and hurt himself. He bonks his head and bruises his knees. I fear the next time it will be worse. These fears create scar tissue in the form of anger and anxiety. I can't keep him from falling. He doesn't always listen. It infuriates me. I just want to keep him SAFE. My anger blossoms in the irrational space where head bumps prove deadly and every regression means he'll grow into an adult who doesn't use utensils. Clearly, I've sailed away from the present.

Marianne Williamson famously says we're either coming from a space of "fear or love." I'm discovering this is true about motherhood. My soul craves calm and order not possible with rice stuck to the wall and mapped out by streaks on the floor. I *fear* it will always be this way.

Enter this super simple mindful breathing hack from Goldie to help me find the love.

"Each time you notice that you have wandered off into thoughts, feelings or sensations, let them go; don't attach to them. See these thoughts as clouds floating across the sky of your mind; then allow them to drift away," Hawn from *"10 Mindful Minutes."*

This powerful visual helped me improve my own mindfulness practice. Here's how: I get Brandon and the baby outside where they'll be distracted. I sit or stand (whatever is possible with the baby in toe) and close my eyes and imagine the ocean. I picture a wave returning to shore and back out to sea with each breath and each exhalation. If I pay attention—the sound of my breathing mimics the sound of wind and water coursing across the sand. I can almost hear the seagulls. Now, for the last week, if I am having a *really* hard time with my son; I visualize him playing happily on the beach as sunlight skips and sparkles for miles. I can float the rest of my day (well, the next twenty minutes or so, in peace).

I'm not saying this is the cure to all of my frustrations. This practice just helps me bounce back from moments of anger much faster. It's nice to know I can go the beach anytime I need. Brandon will outgrow the trying-two's. After dinner, the other night Brandon said "Thank you mommy, cooking." He didn't use his spoon but he did use his manners. He's a good boy. I'm trying really hard to be the mommy he deserves. It just takes practice.

26 Questions to Ask When Life Gets Hard

I sighed deeply. *Why is everything so hard?* Well, for starters my two-month old daughter and I spent two days in the hospital after a terrifying mid-night choking spell. My absence hurt my two-year-old son's feelings (feelings, already so very bruised and banged from the arrival of his sister). As I try to make it up to him (by taking him all over town to go to play-dates and story time WITH A BABY) I exhaust myself. He rewards me by darting onto an escalator. Somehow I scoop him up as he whines, hollers and narrowly escapes a terrible tumble. I cling to both of my babies and my sanity as we climb to the top of a Barnes & Noble. Did I mention I just released a book? An e-book chalked full of lessons, affirmations and takeaways about reporting, motherhood, staying present and learning to enjoy life. It's sold an unlucky 13 copies. I feel defeated. I am sure you've felt this way too. So, after the big question: WHY IS EVERYTHING SO HARD? Here are some follow ups I must ask myself. Maybe you can give them a whirl the next time you're feeling overwhelmed by life.

1. ARE YOU TAKING CARE OF YOURSELF? This is a biggie. On this particular week I might give myself a C+. I stole some time to stretch, and give myself a nighttime massage on Tuesday. Otherwise, I feel as worn as old bowling shoes and my eye is twitching.
2. ARE YOU TRYING TO DO TOO MUCH? I think you know my answer to this one.

3. WHAT'S YOUR INNER-DIALOUGE LIKE? In my late twenties I spent a lot of time in the self-help aisle at Barnes and talking through my inner-dialogue with a therapist. I cannot allow myself to believe mean thoughts about myself or my work. I am a work in progress just like everybody else. This was especially important this week given the lackluster sales and my epic moments in motherhood gone awry.
4. ARE YOU IN *AND MAINTAINING* HEALTHY RELATIONSHIPS? The answer is yes. However, this was not always the case especially in my twenties. I've learned healthy relationships are the cornerstone of life.
5. HOW ARE YOU NURTURING YOUR CREATIVITY? This week my creativity turned cannibalistic feeding on my worries and gnawing on my sense of confidence. Good question! I will focus some attention here.
6. ARE YOU DRINKING ENOUGH WATER AND EATING HEALTHY FOODS? Eating good healthy foods makes me feel better. The burger I ate on Friday didn't do me any favors. A tall glass of water right now just might help with my headache.
7. HOW ARE YOU SLEEPING? I need my inner-beauty sleep like whoa.
8. WHEN WAS THE LAST TIME YOU HAD SEX? I won't answer that. But yes, *it's that important*.
9. HOW ARE YOU EXERCISING? Walking? Running? Swimming? Nope, it's time to tackle this one too.
10. DO YOU MAKE ROOM IN YOUR LIFE FOR YOUR DREAMS? Yes, I think so. Although, right now they're hazy and evolving.

11. WHAT KIND OF RISKS ARE YOU TAKING? Putting myself out there was a big risk and I am proud of myself for stepping outside of my comfort zone.
12. ARE YOU TOO CONCERNED WITH OUTSIDE VALIDATION? I must answer an unflattering, yep. Even though, I don't want to be overly concerned with outside validation. Again I am a work in progress. I wrote my book for myself and for my children. It was my therapy when I was going through my new mommy identity crisis. I don't need accolades. I need to celebrate this great time in my life.
13. ARE YOU FEELING JEALOUS? Jealousy is a difficult emotion for me to own up to. However, it's important. If I catch myself feeling jealous I must use the feeling to help me identify qualities I want to bring to my life. After I learn from my feelings I can release them. Denise Duffield Thomas, Author of *Get Rich Lucky Bitch* says if you're feeling jealous put your hands on your heart and say "good things are happening for me too."
14. ARE YOU ENJOYING THE PROCESS OF LIFE? Too often I wish away the everyday. I can't do that now. I have two little ones who change every, single, glorious day. They hold me accountable to enjoying the process.
15. ARE YOU STAYING PRESENT? Once again, my babies hold me accountable to the process and most certainly the moment.
I too often get sucked into the world in my phone or a book or my worries. I can't wander away from what's so wonderful right in front of me. I say it in the book, "Deep breaths are free all day long."

16. ARE YOU GRATEFUL? Of course I am so very grateful for the ride (maybe not up the escalator) but this life is amazing.
17. ARE YOU LEARNING? It is important for me to take time to learn. I love learning new things and when I stop learning my brain cells grow mutinous and turn on each other. Also, when life is really hard I must accept that there's something to learn.
18. HOW'S YOUR FINANCIAL HEALTH? Money buys options. My bank account can only bend so far before I feel like I'm running out of options and I'm going to break. A plan helps to ease my anxiety.
19. IS YOUR HOUSE/PURSE/DESK/CAR CLEAN? Organization makes life a little easier. Yay, for not finding goldfish at the bottom of your purse.
20. ARE YOU HAVING FUN? This week, not so much. Yet, I found a few little giggle crumbs, to hold me over, while bouncing my daughter on my lap.
21. DO YOU FIND WAYS TO PAMPER YOURSELF? I am a mother of two. Obviously I need to work on this.
22. DO YOU FEEL FABULOUS? Again, I might need to dust off the blow dryer and pull out the Spanx. Feeling good on the outside can shoot good vibes inside.
23. WHAT'S YOUR VICE? Right now it's technology but during my younger days I dealt with different vices. However, no matter the vice its best if it's kept in check.

24. DO YOU NEED TO MAKE A CHANGE OR JUST REFRAME? Sometimes, life is just hard. (If you're going through a divorce or caring for a sick loved-one.) I've read stats suggesting parents of young children actually see a dip in happiness. Mothering little ones feels a lot like treading water off the coast of a gorgeous private island. It's a gorgeous view but exhausting and scary. In my case, I don't need to make a change. I just need to reframe my experience. Let's call this *the learning and development* phase of my life. Maybe you need to make a change? Either way it's an important question.
25. ARE YOU GIVING TO OTHERS? I know when I do something with a friend or stranger in mind, I feel better about myself.
26. HOW'S YOUR REALTIONSHIP WITH GOD/THE UNIVERSE/THE QUIET AT DAWN? I think it's important to ask yourself how you feel when the lights go out. Can I dwell in the quiet without reaching for the world outside of myself or do I immediately go searching for the light by way of the closest gadget. A random google search can't replace a little soul-searching. *Amen! Okay, I need to work on this one too. Why is everything so hard?* Too often, it's because I am not drinking enough water or taking time for myself. I hope by searching for the answers to these follow up questions I can kick the feeling of overwhelm. How about you? Would you add any more to the list?

The End

Made in the USA
Coppell, TX
31 December 2023